Justin Perkins

Hiatus

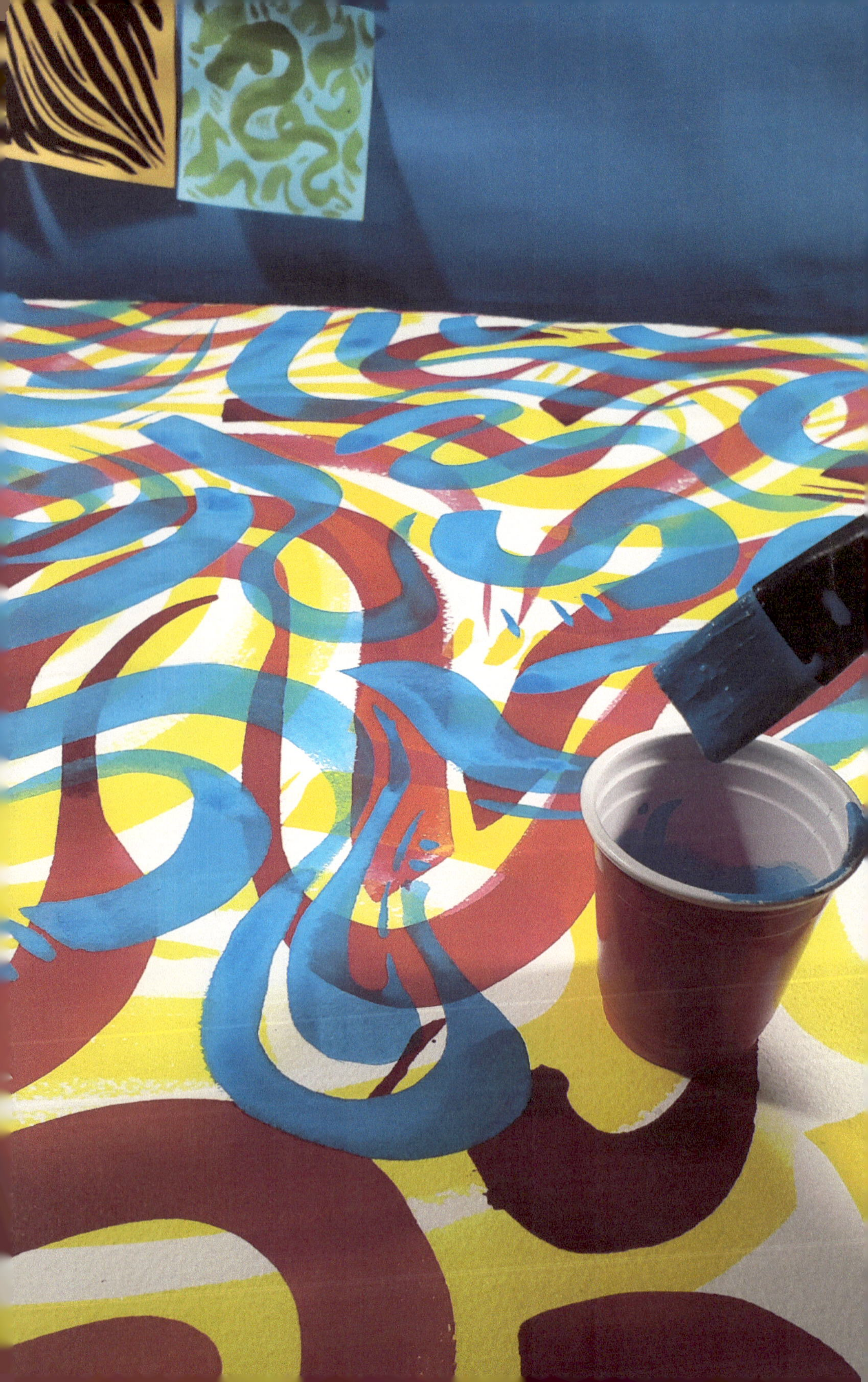

Hiatus
Published by J Perkins Art LLC

jperkinsart.com

ISBN
978-1-7360110-0-3

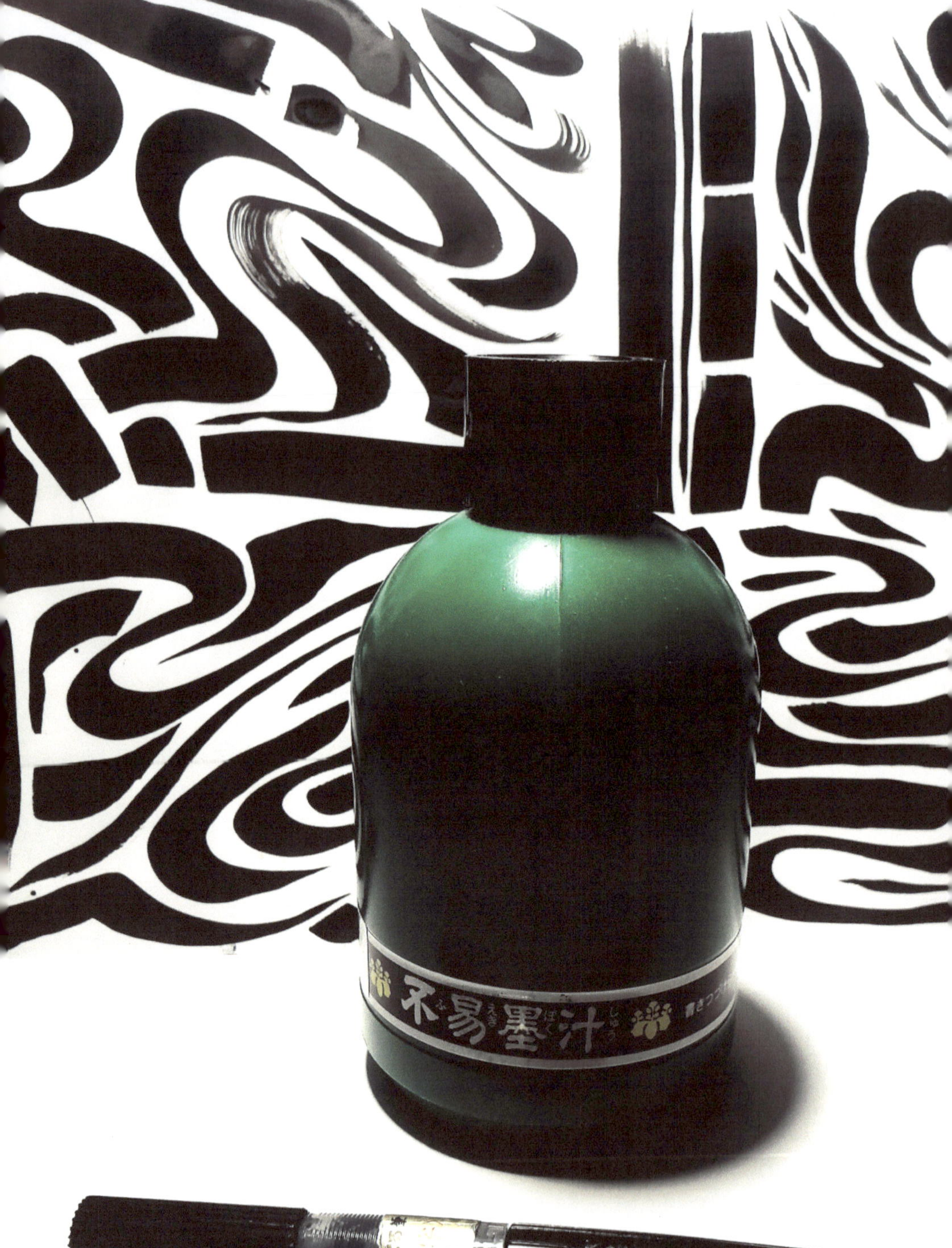
不易墨汁

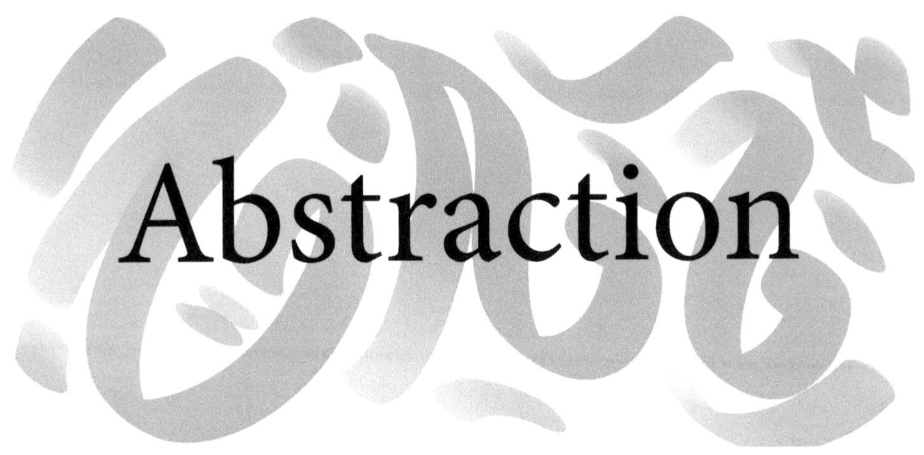

Abstraction

Although I admired abstract artists and their work. I didn't think about creating my own abstract artwork very often. My only experience with it was a few sculptures while I was in art school and examples while I was teaching my elementary school art students. Without me noticing I got into the habit of making marks and patterns in my sketchbooks. It started with just marks to test out new brush pens and inks, then it evolved to making marks around doodles as a background to plain looking sketches. Eventually I started filling whole pages with these abstract marks and patterns.

When I finally decided to explore this fascination with brush strokes it was a very interesting experience. For a long time I had been trying to show the unique qualities of the mediums I used in my artwork and give them a more prominent role in the images I create. I'm not certain if doing abstract artwork is the answer to what I have been looking for, or if it is a steeping stone in my eternal art education. Either way it has been a very freeing and fulfilling experience.

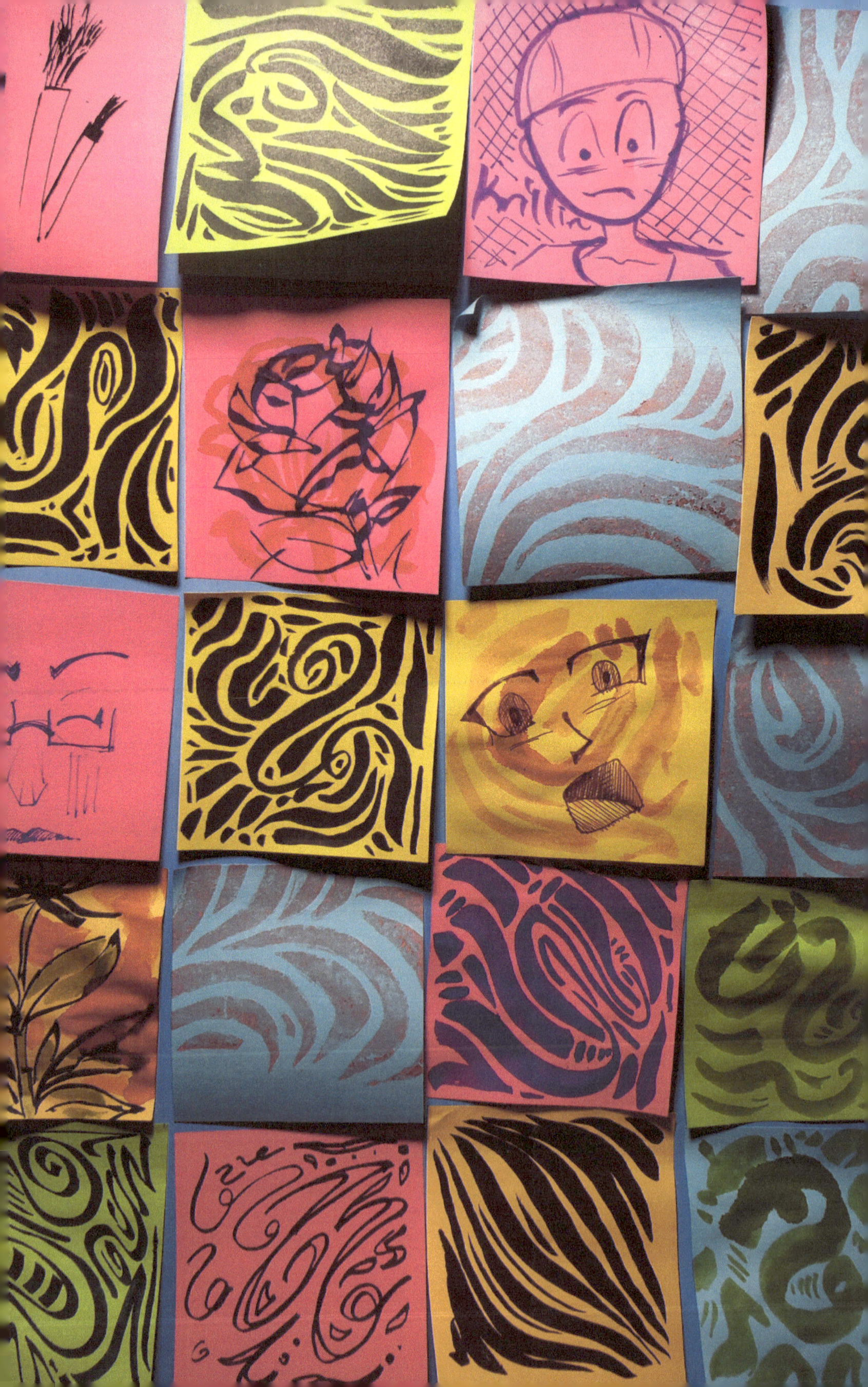

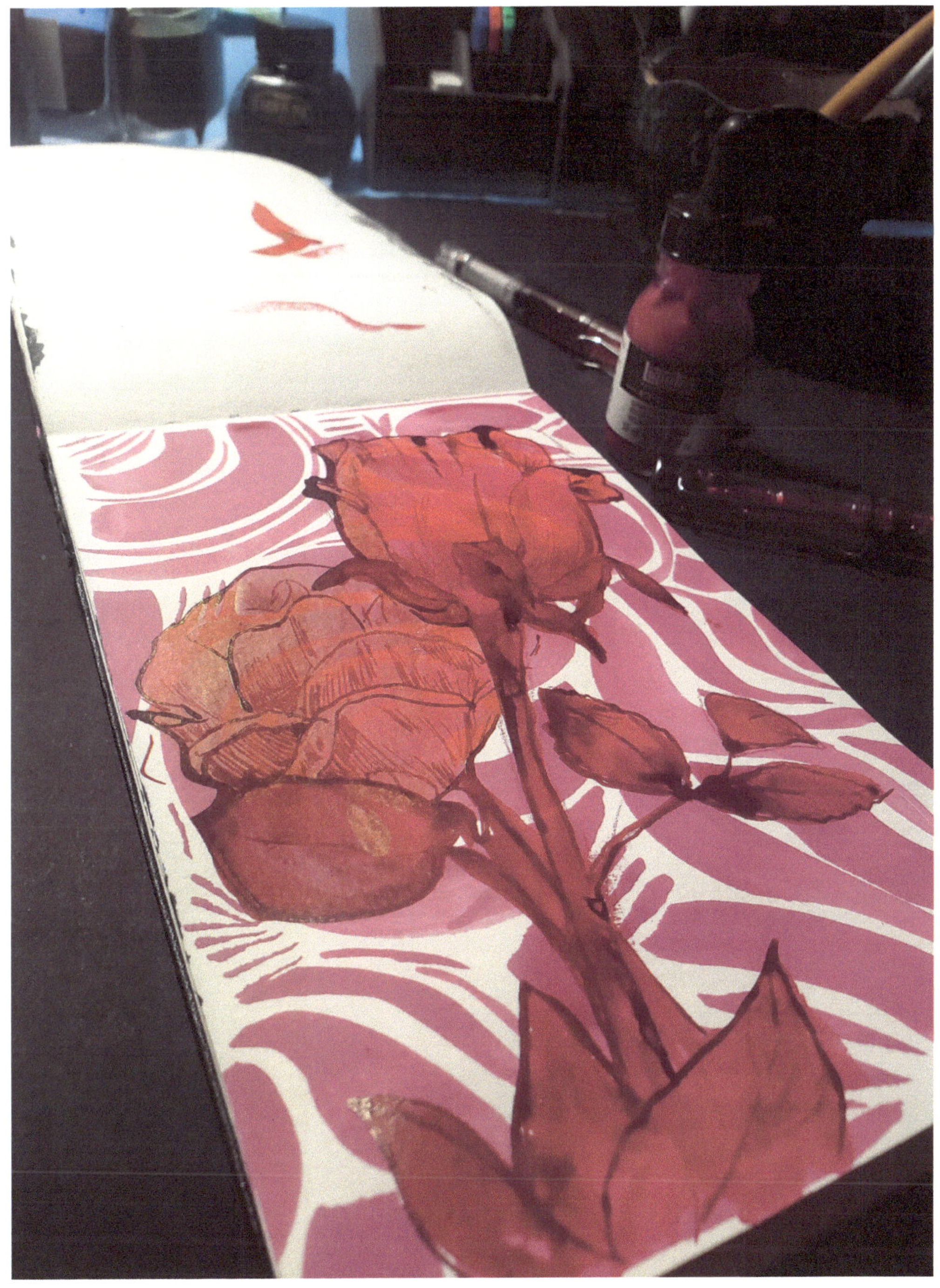

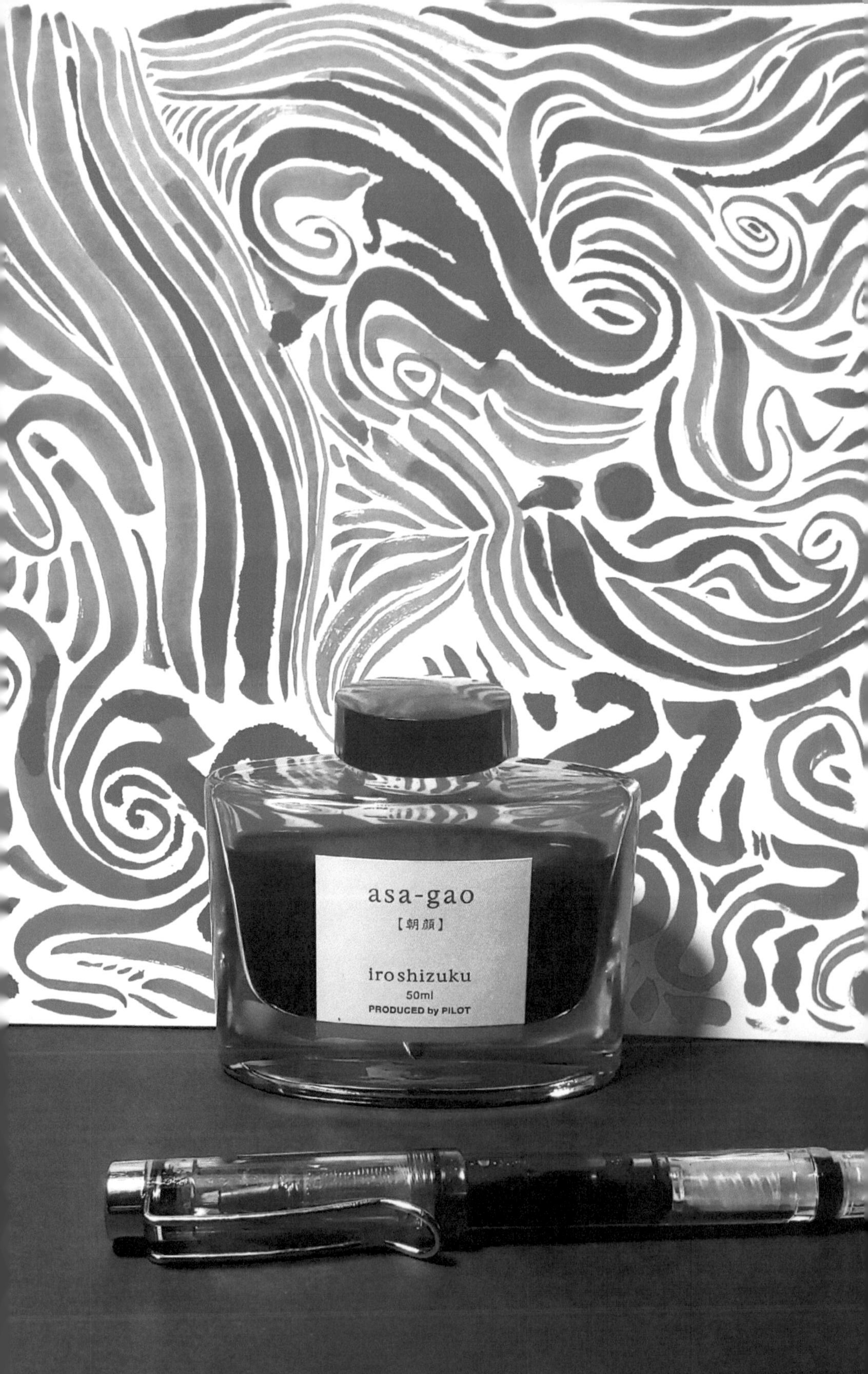
asa-gao
【朝顔】
iroshizuku
50ml
PRODUCED by PILOT

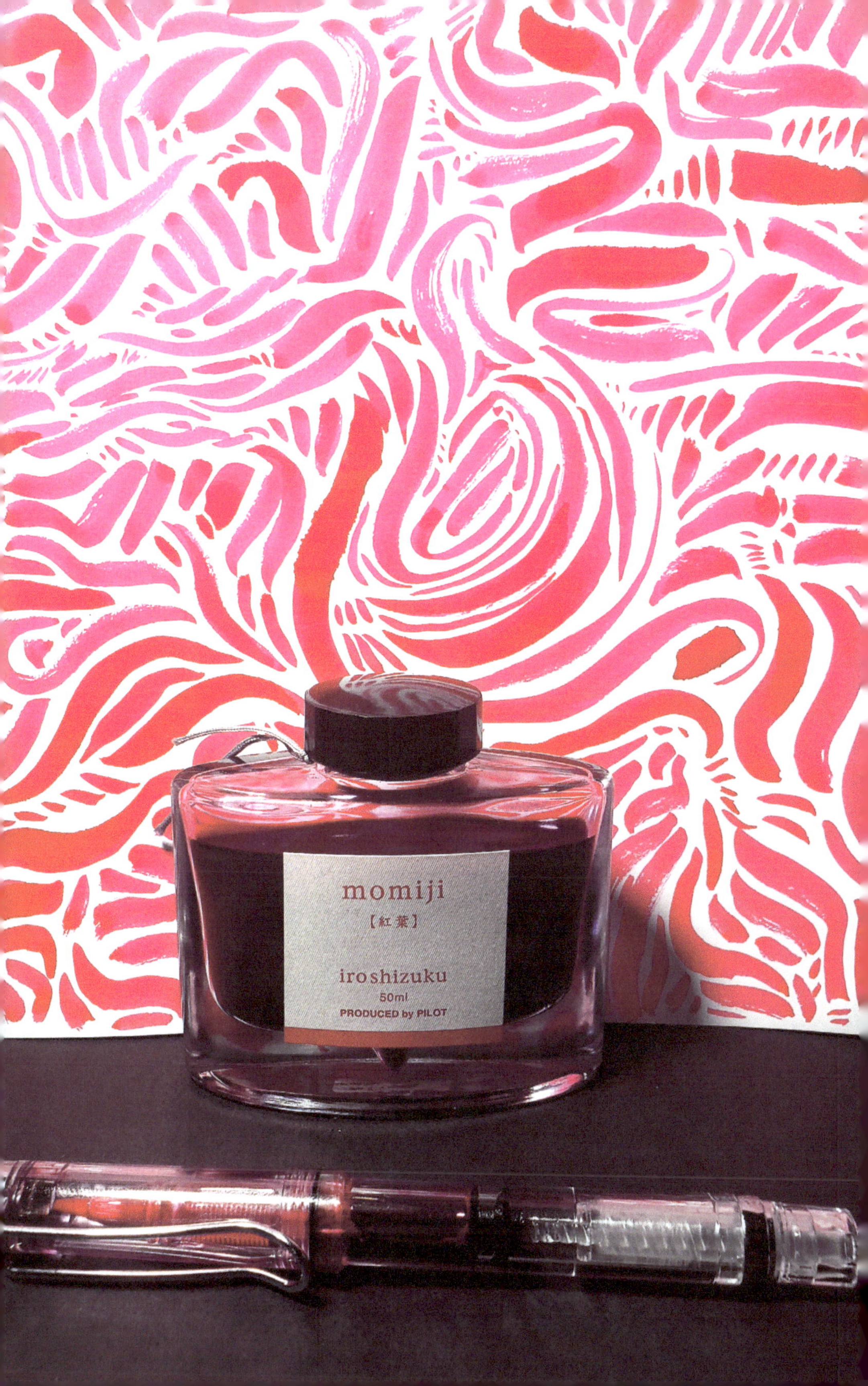
momiji
【紅葉】
iroshizuku
50ml
PRODUCED by PILOT

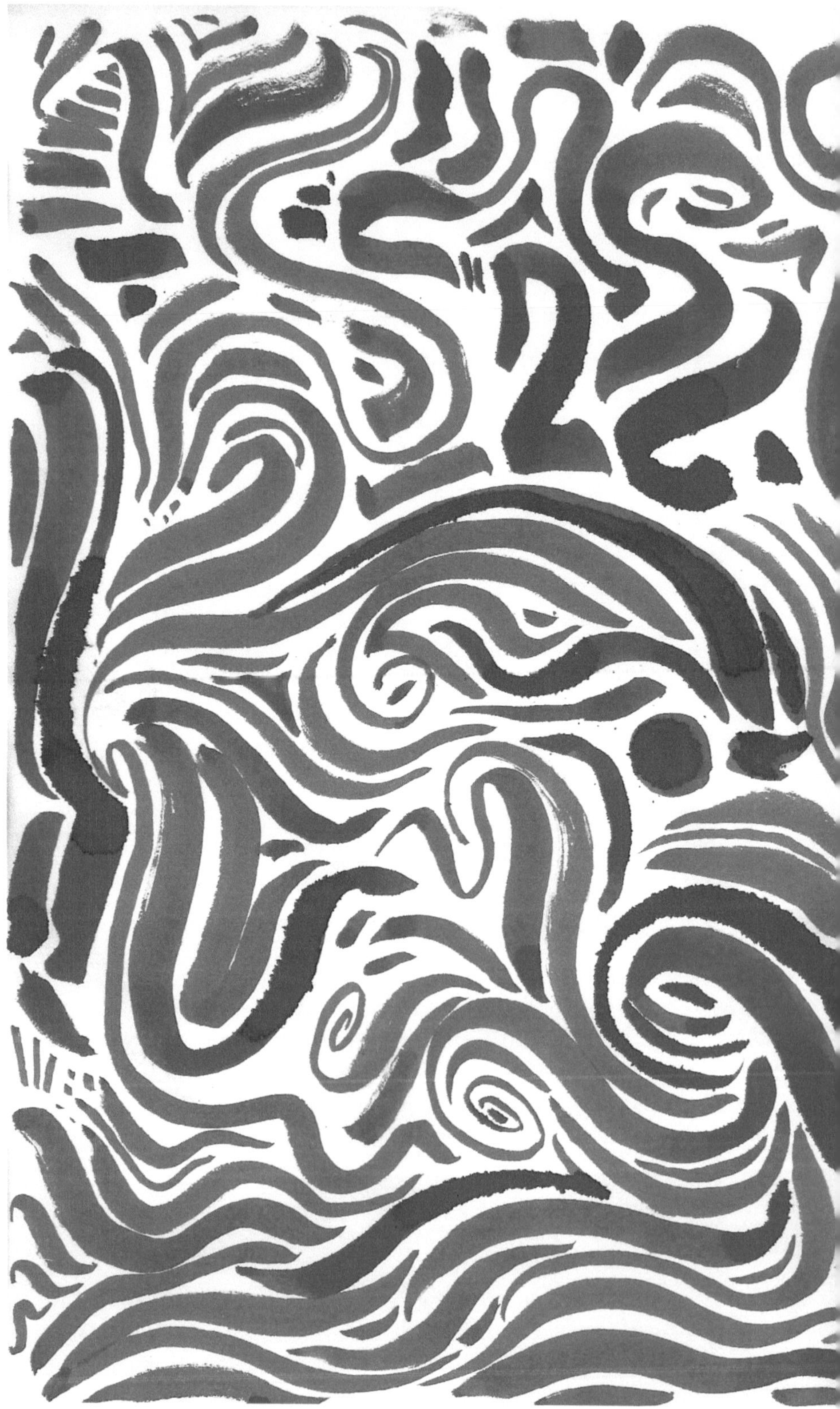

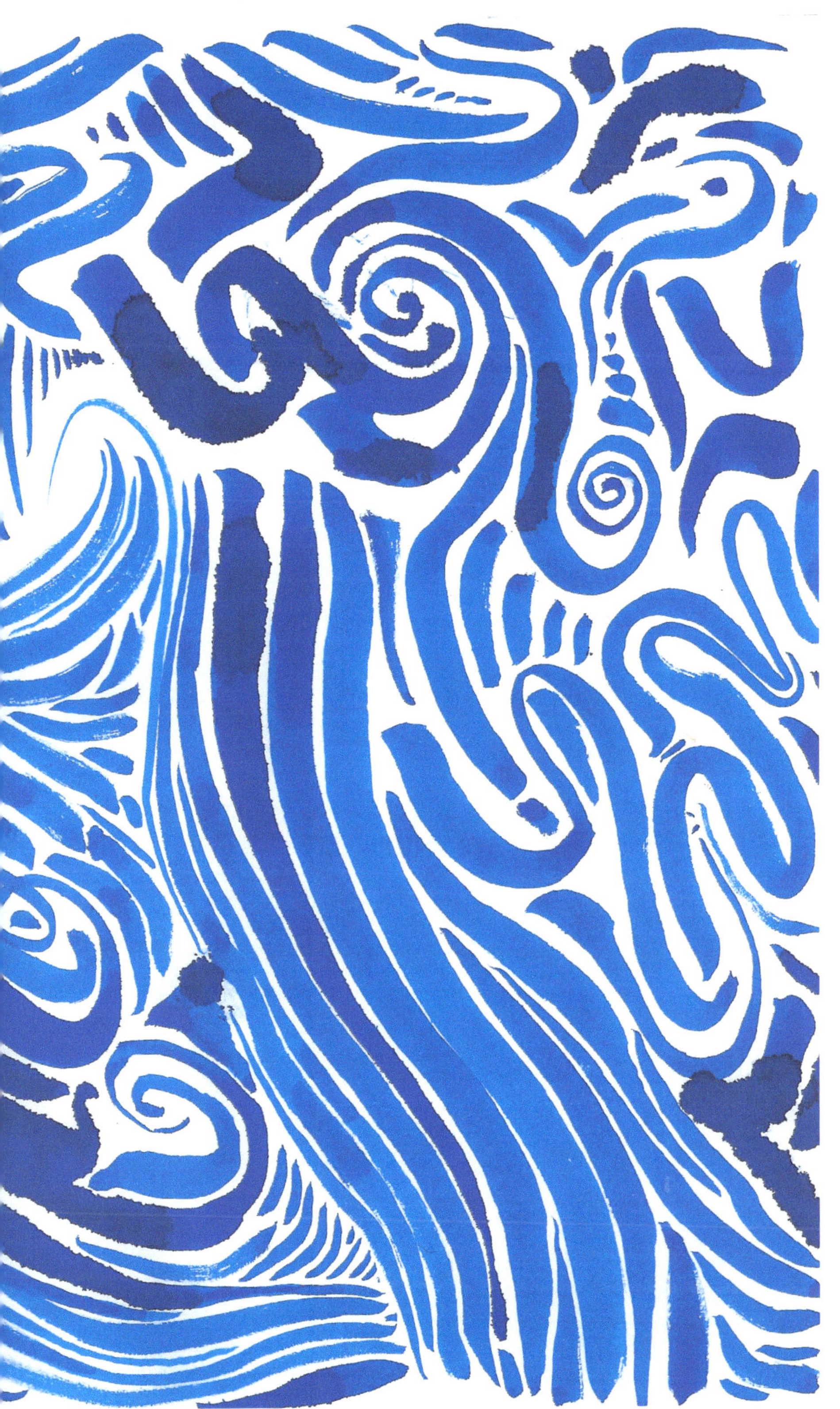

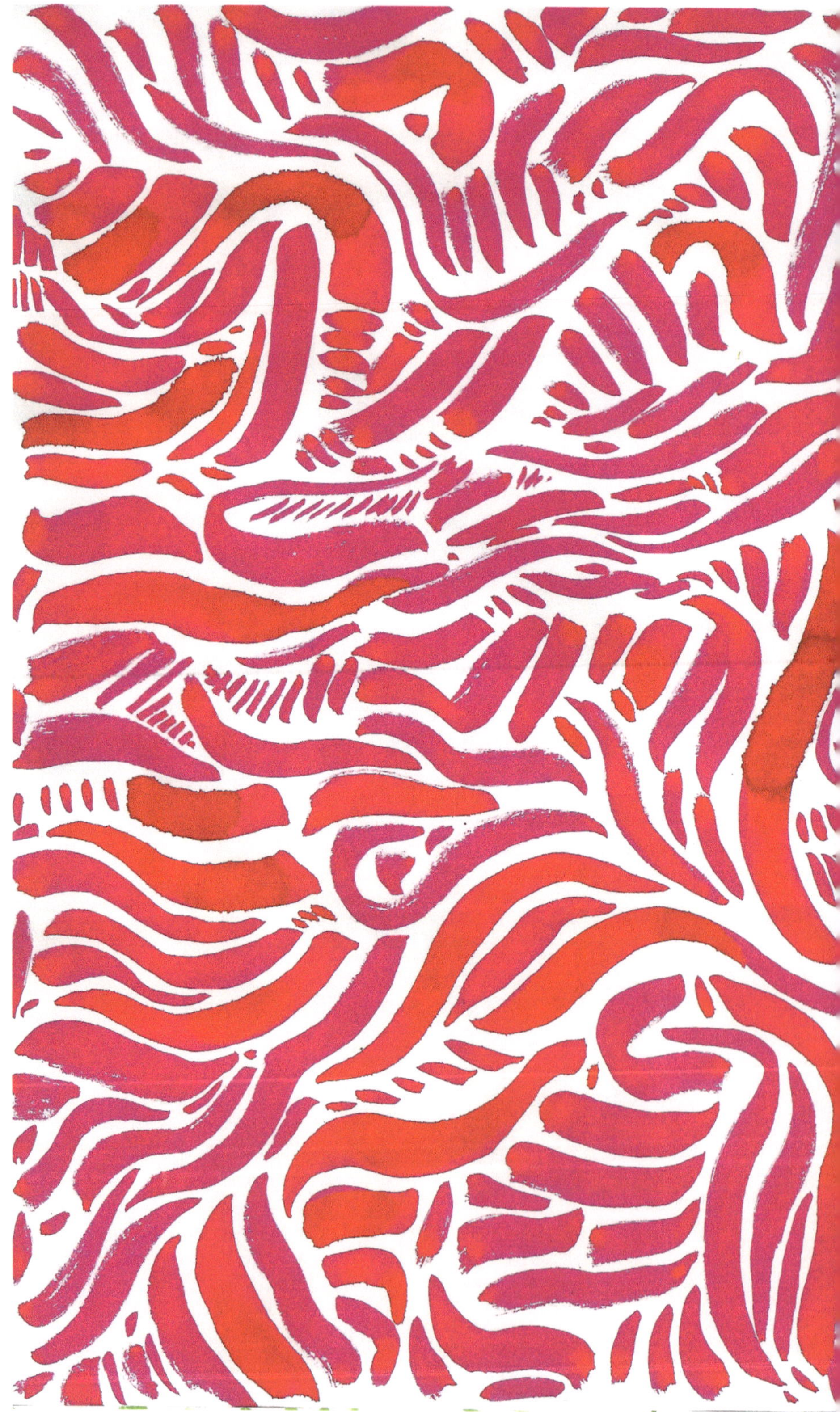

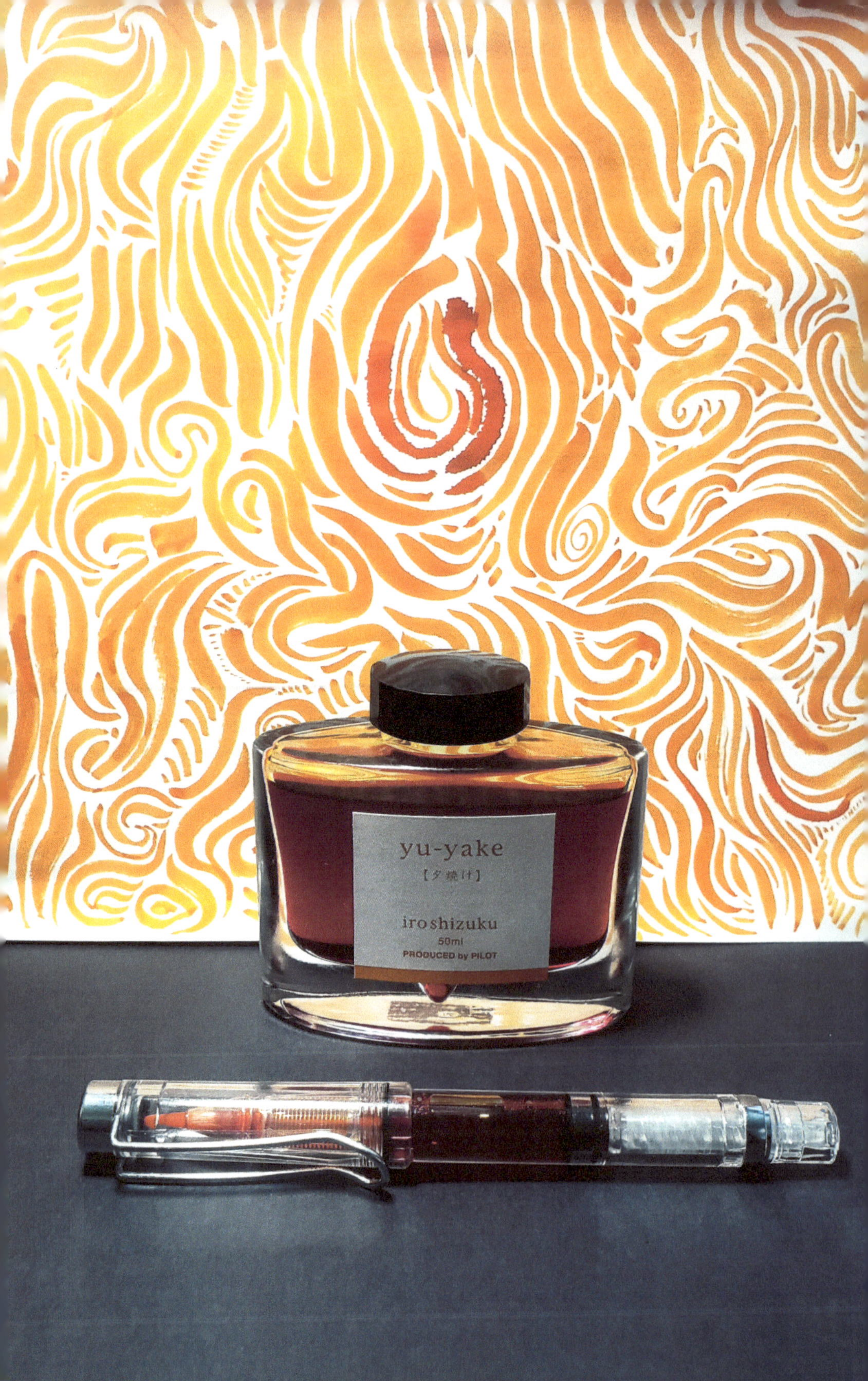
yu-yake
【夕焼け】
iroshizuku
50ml
PRODUCED by PILOT

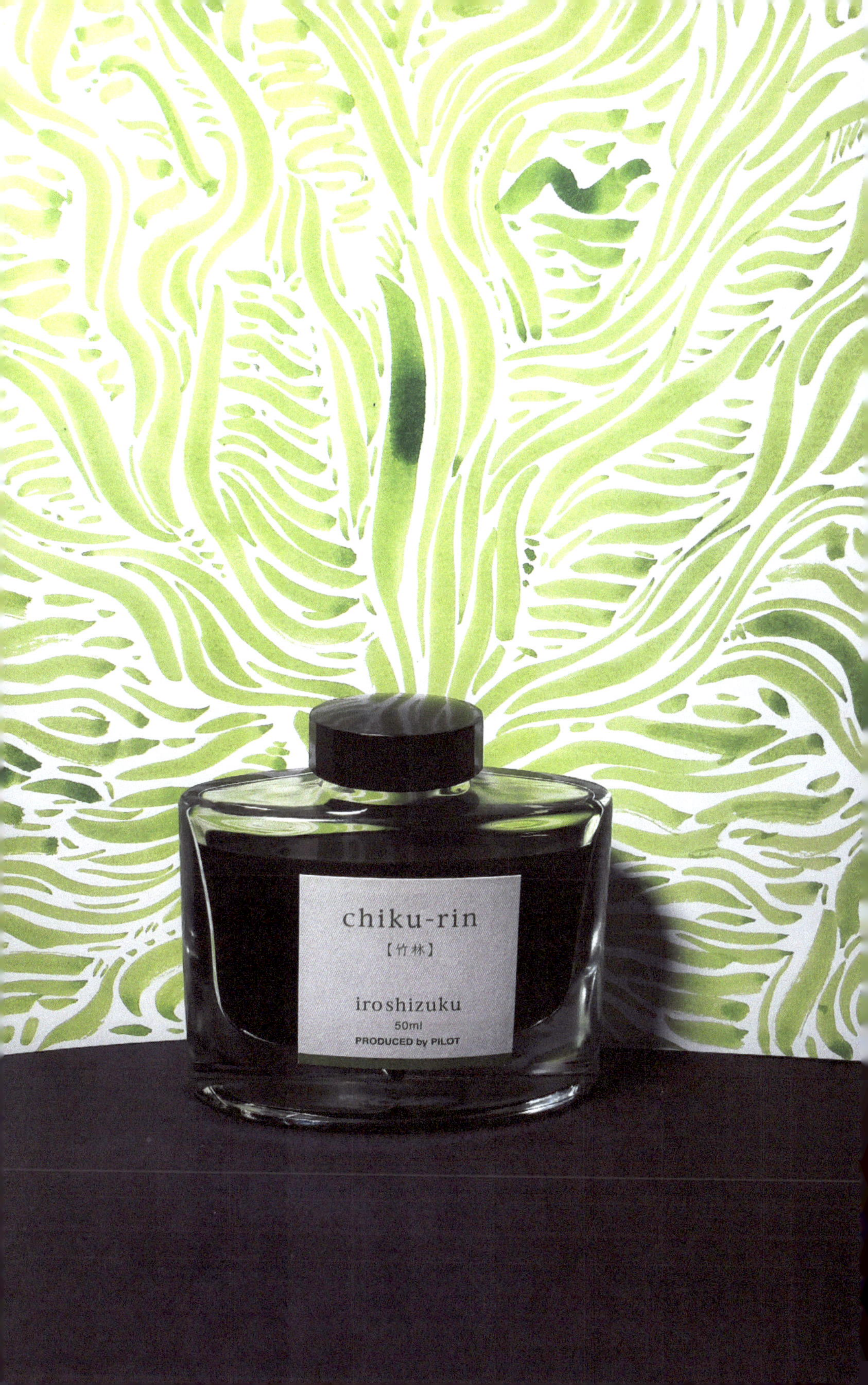
chiku-rin
【竹林】
iroshizuku
50ml
PRODUCED by PILOT

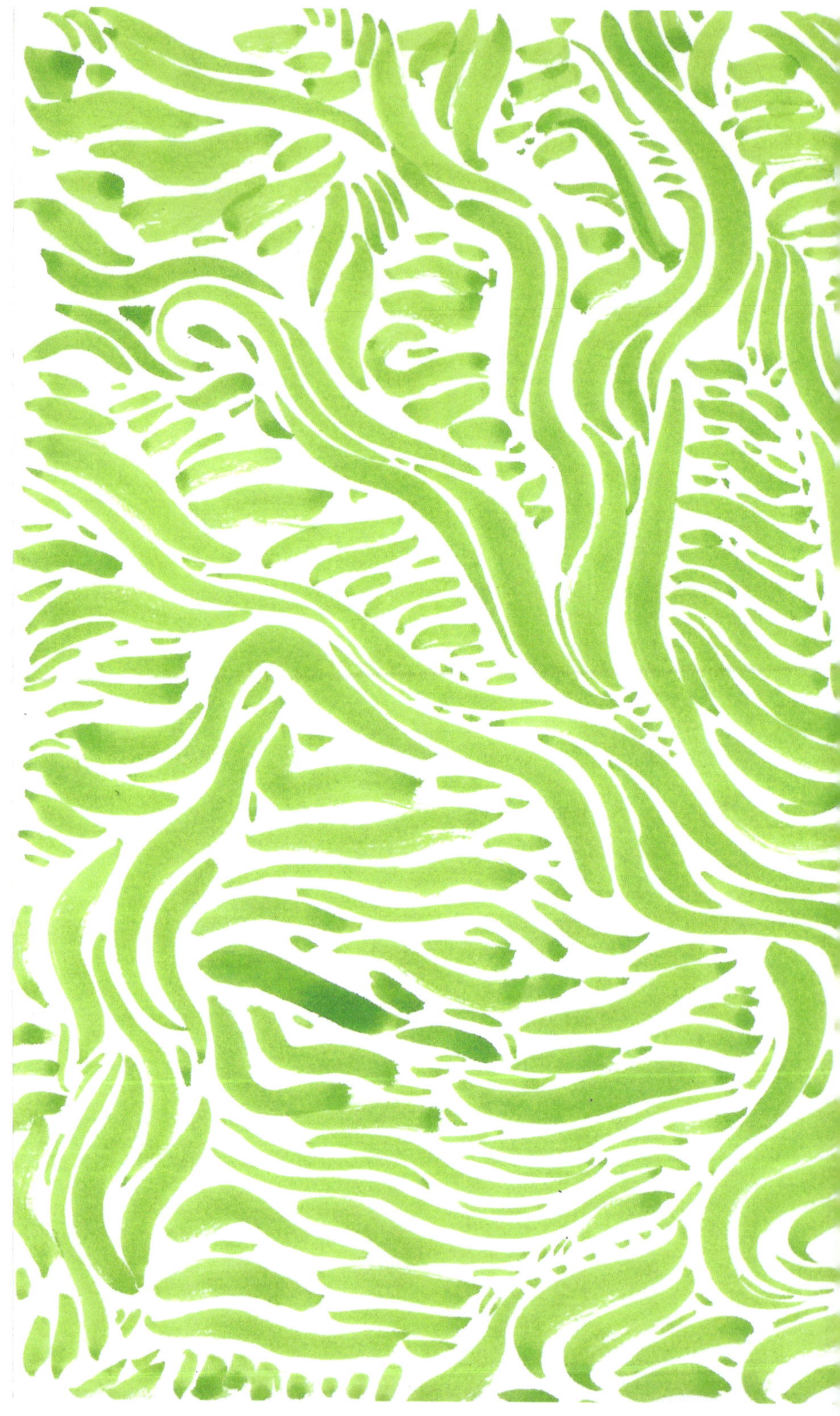

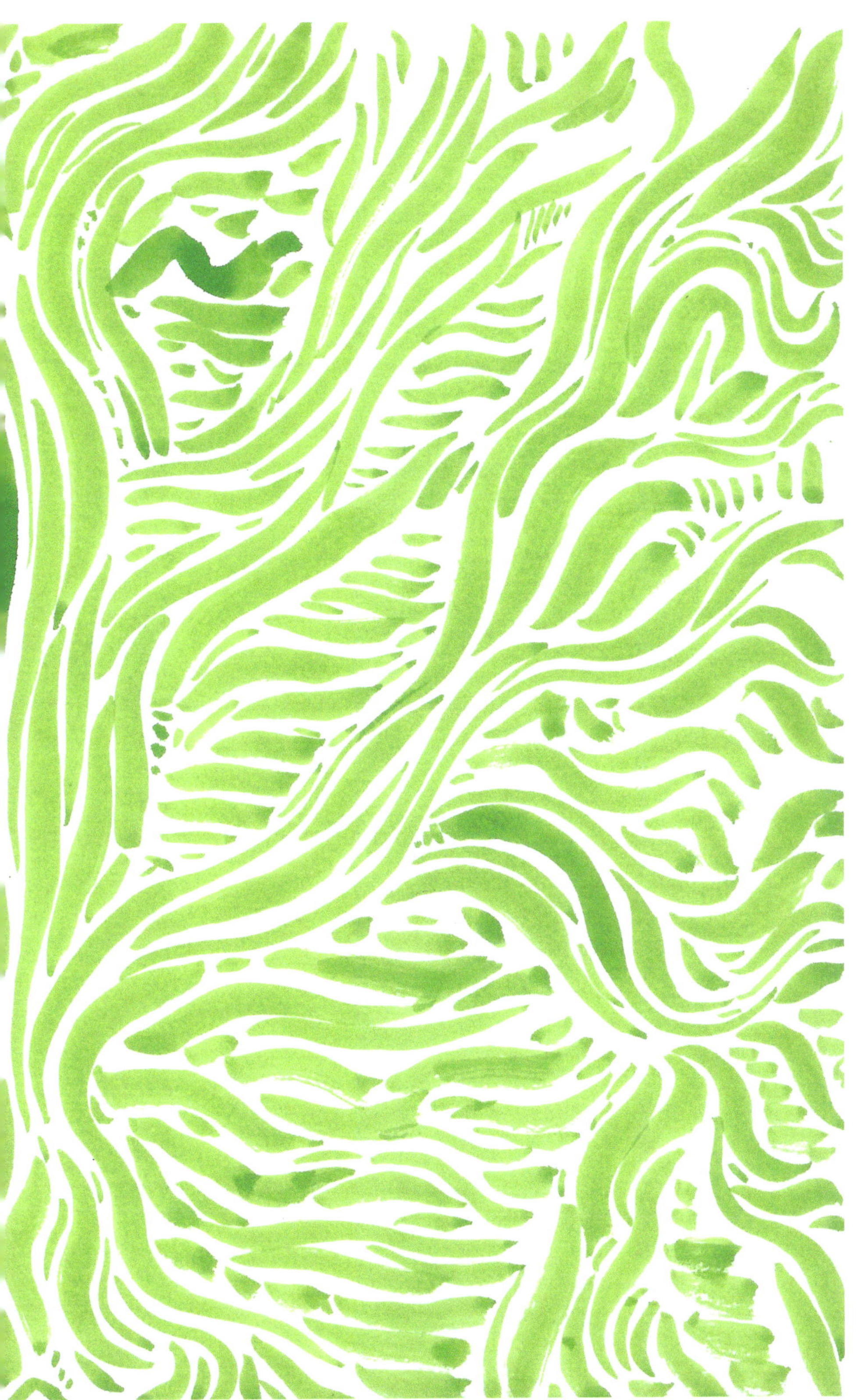

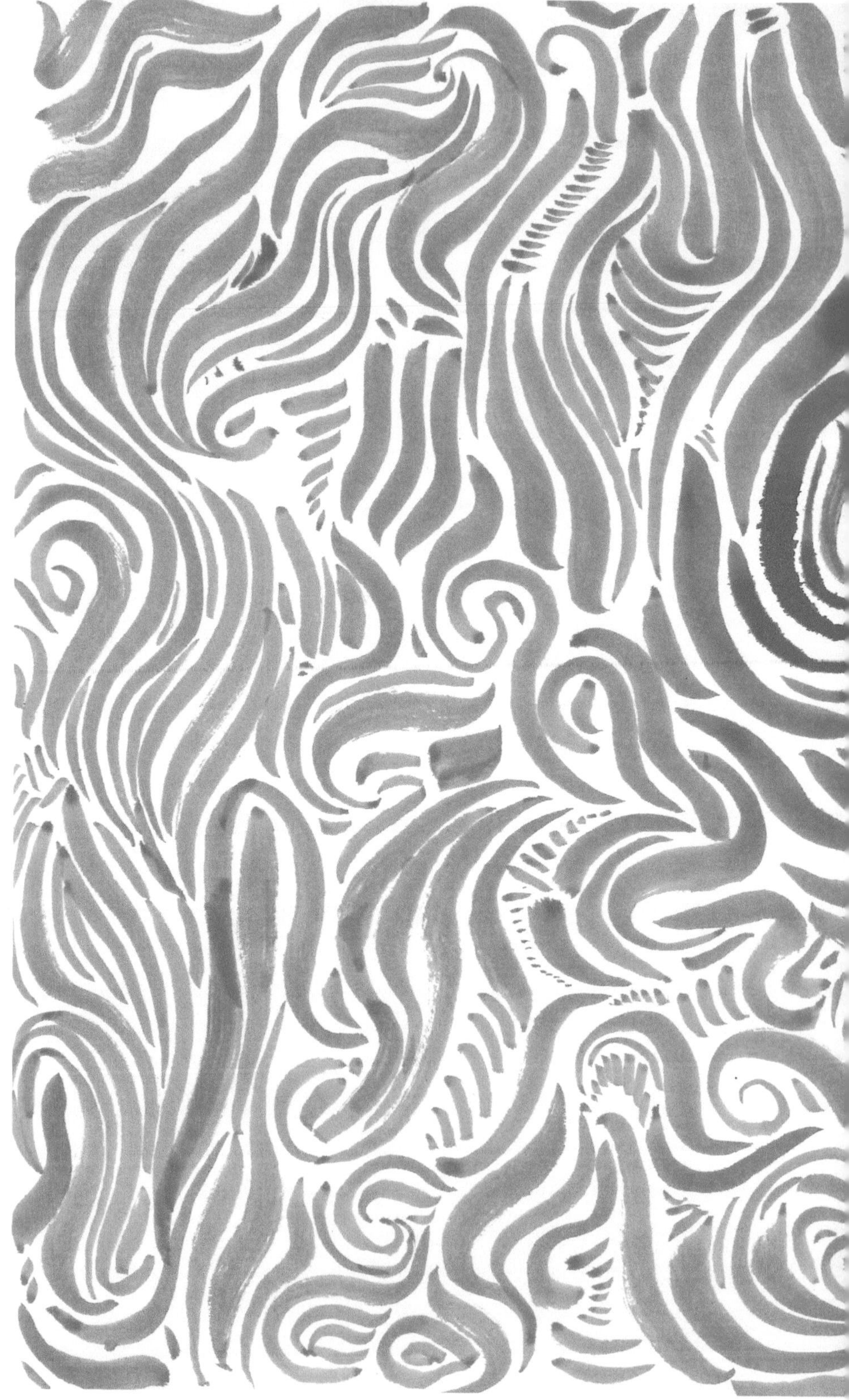

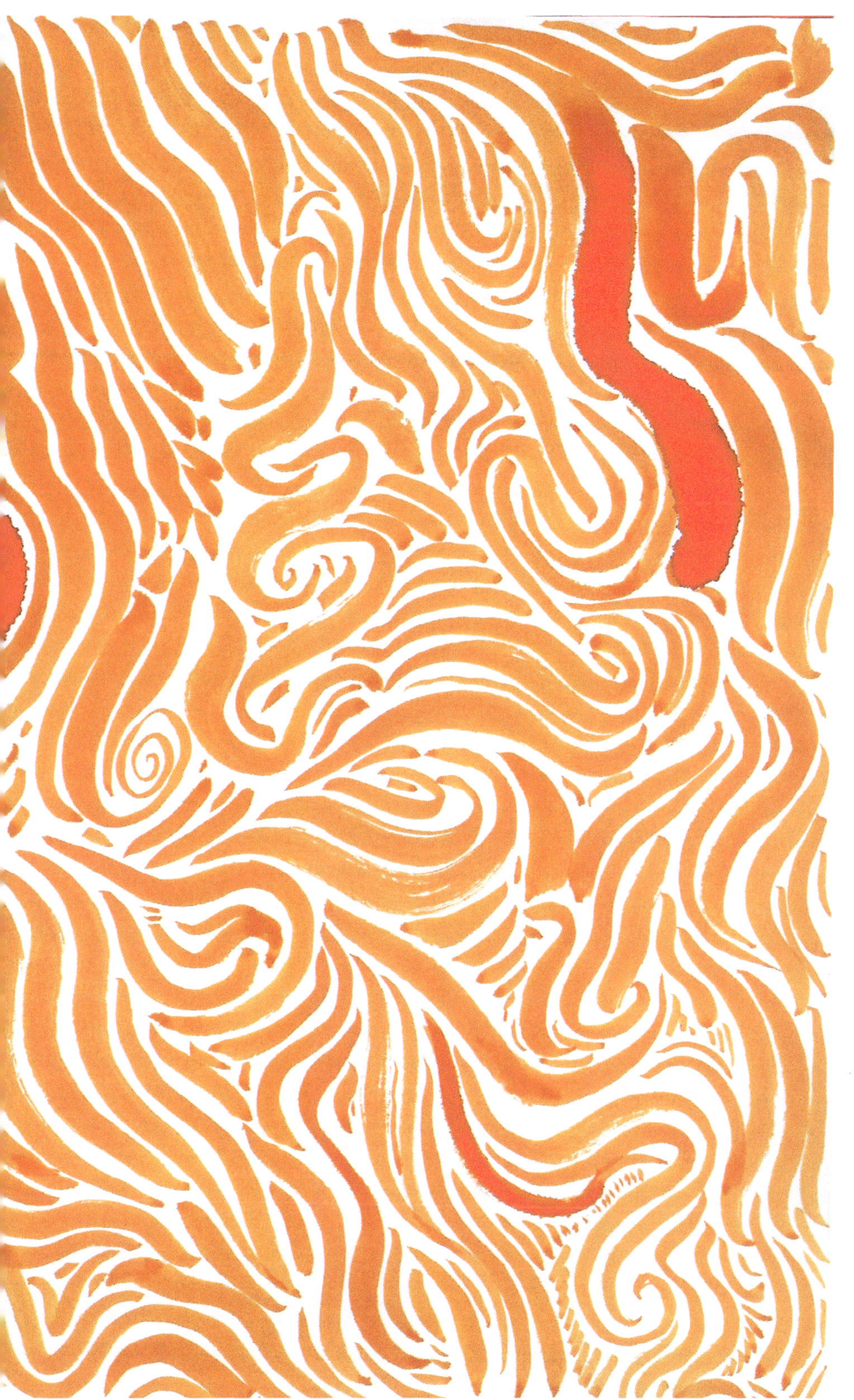

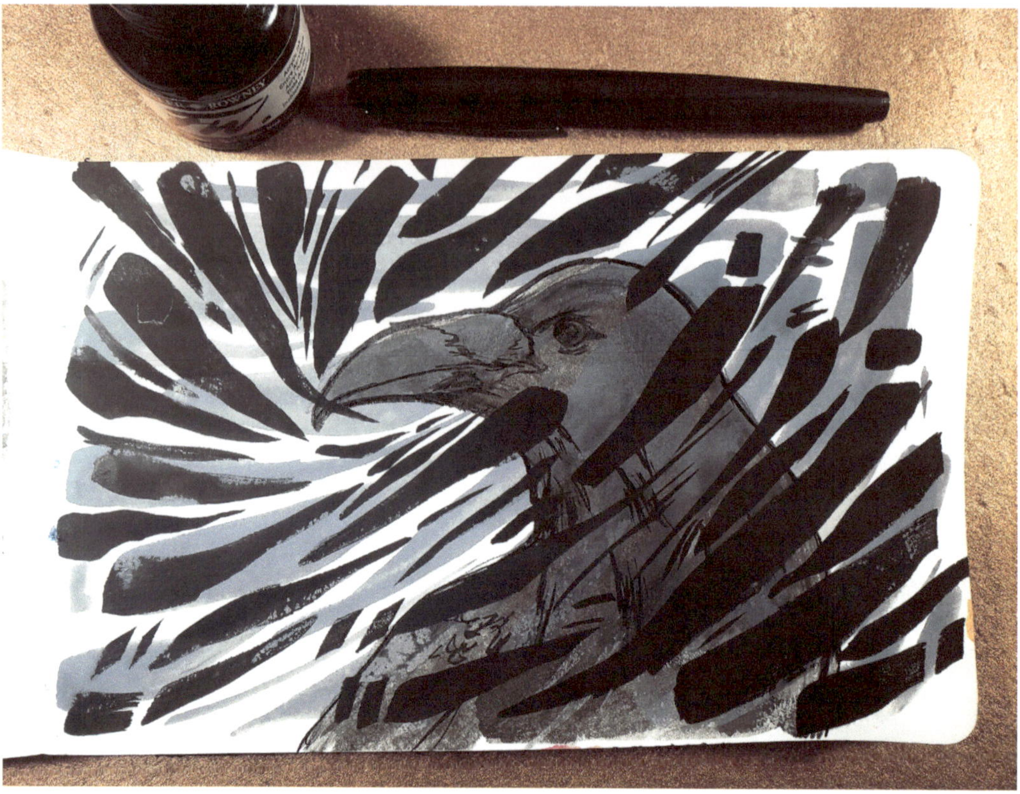

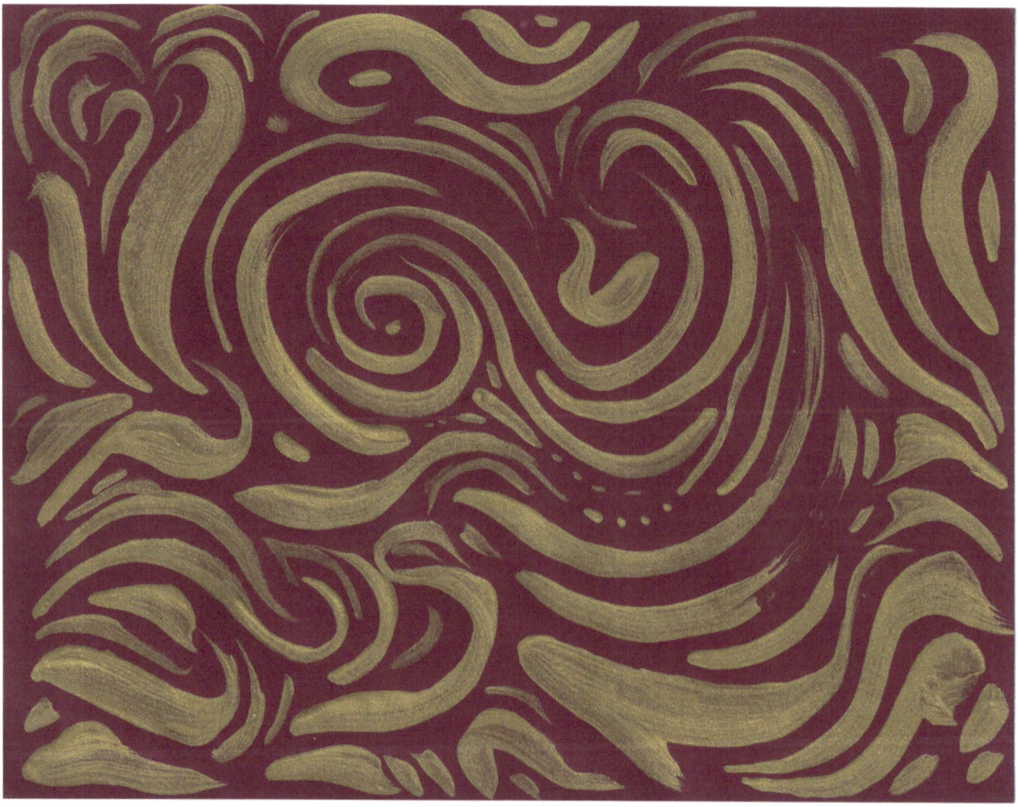

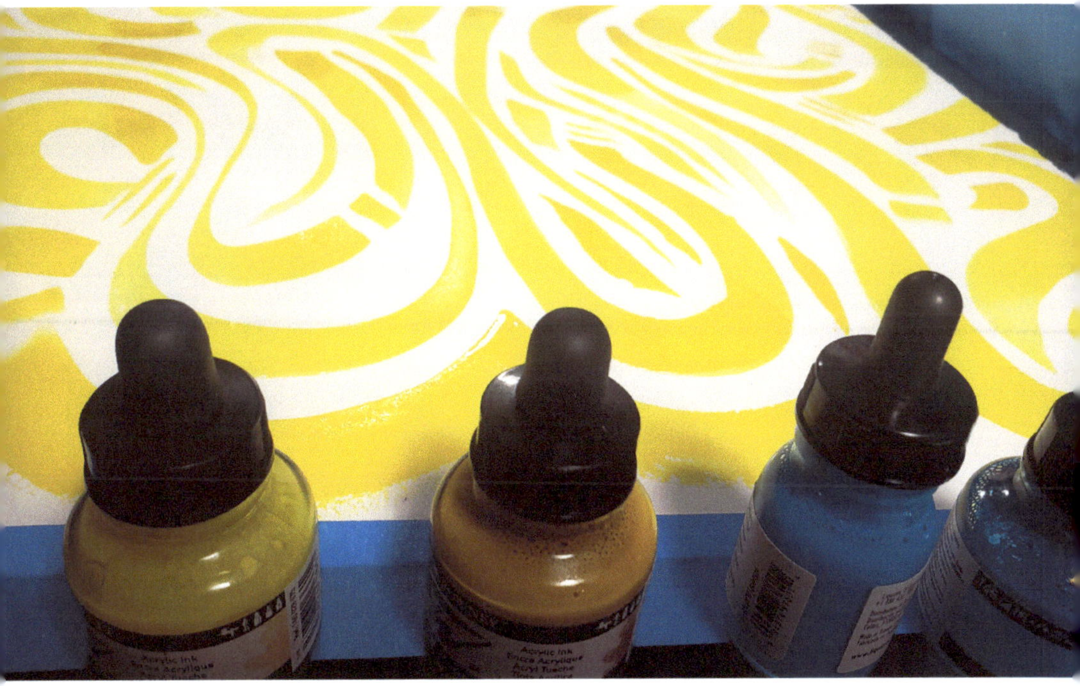

Acrylic Ink
Encre Acrylique
Acryl Tusche

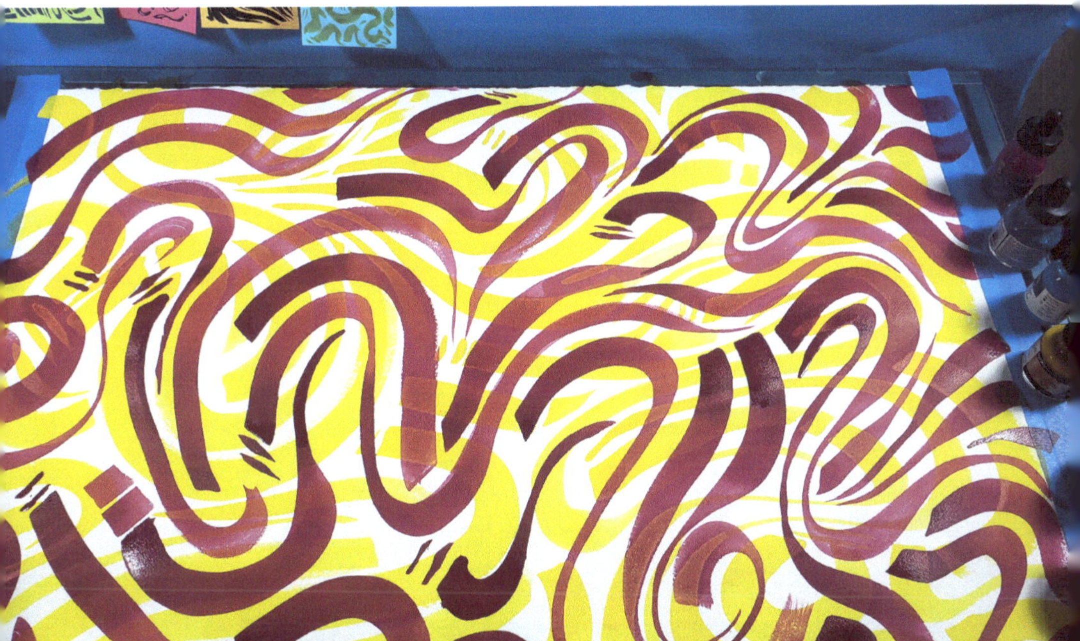

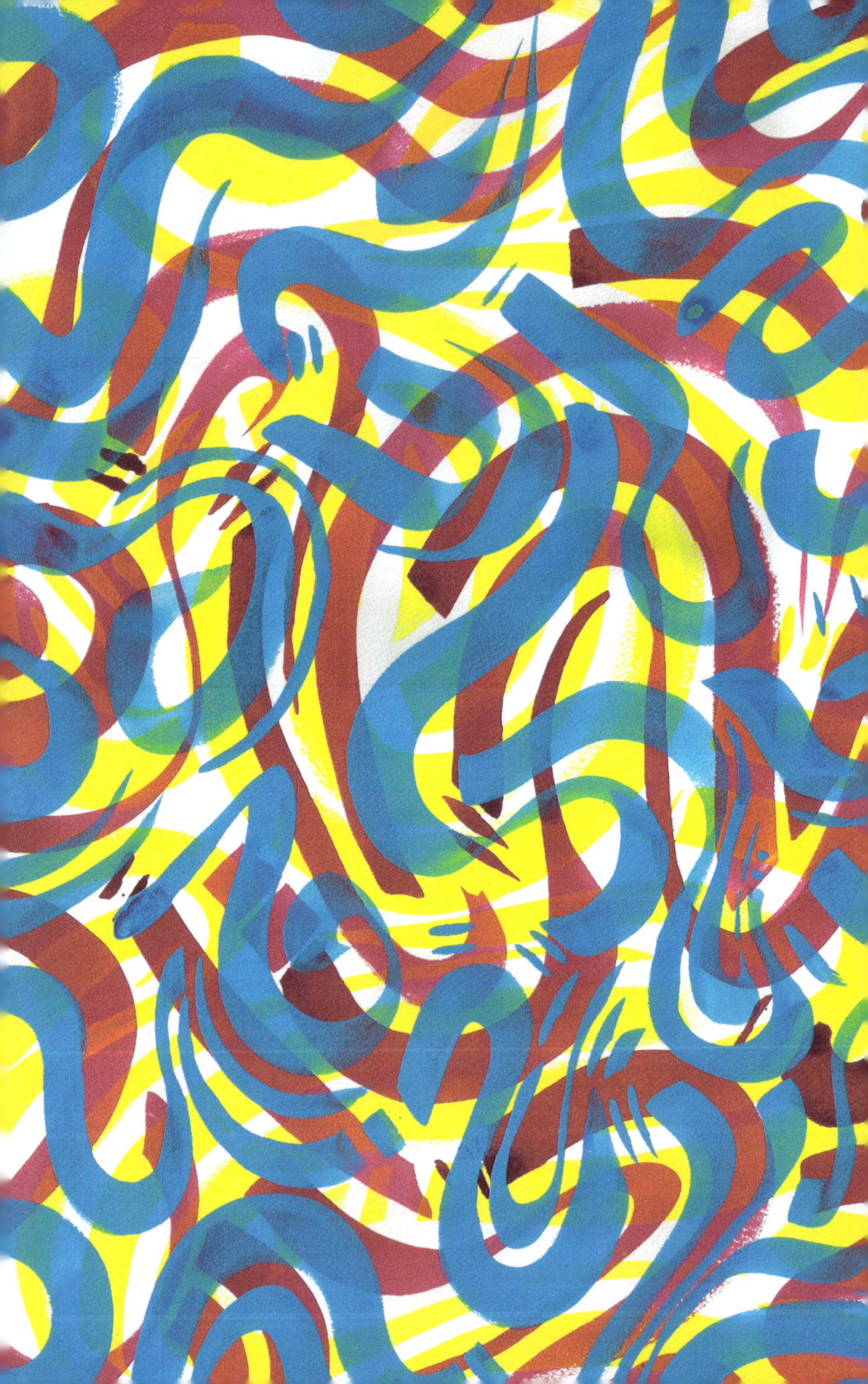

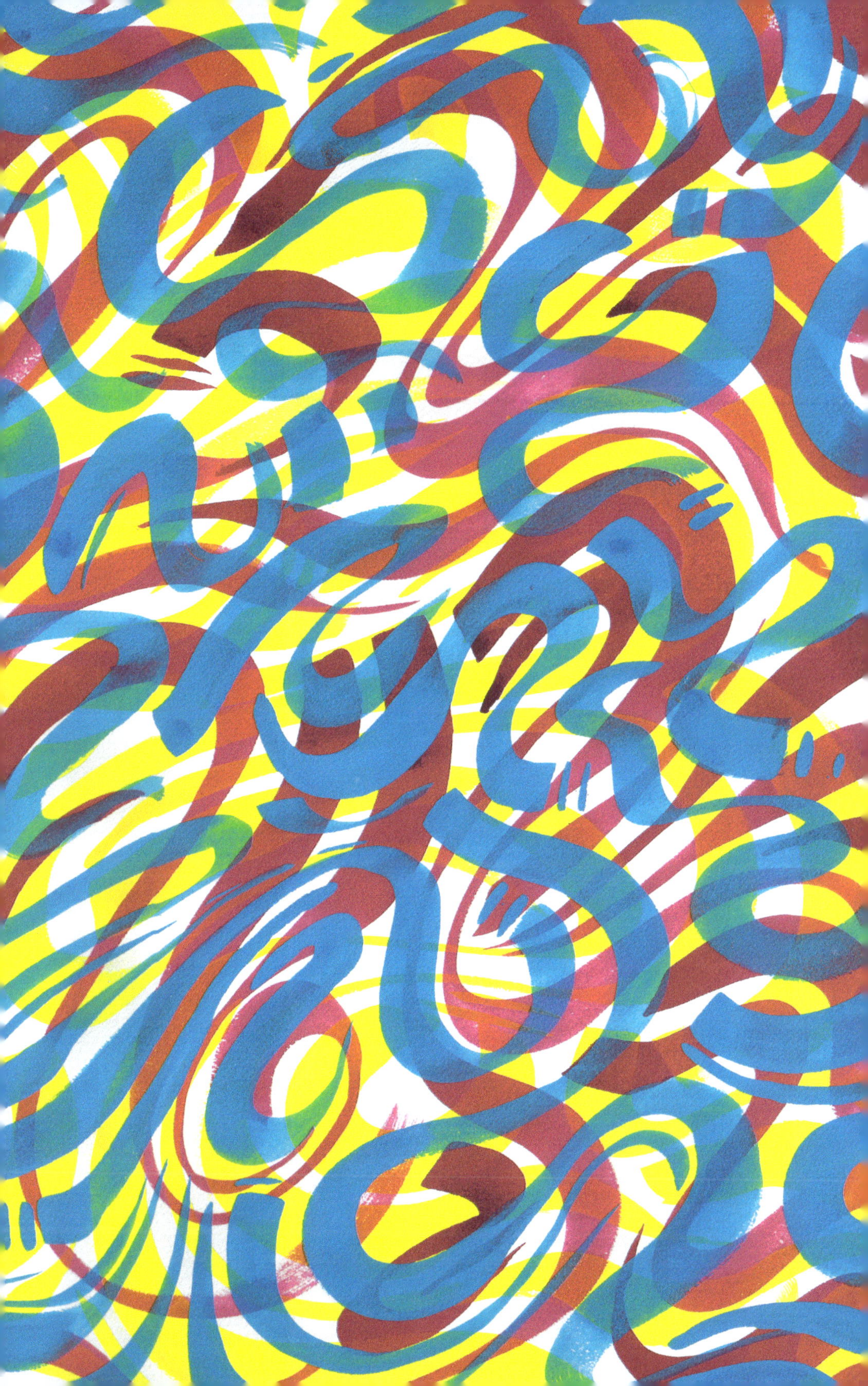

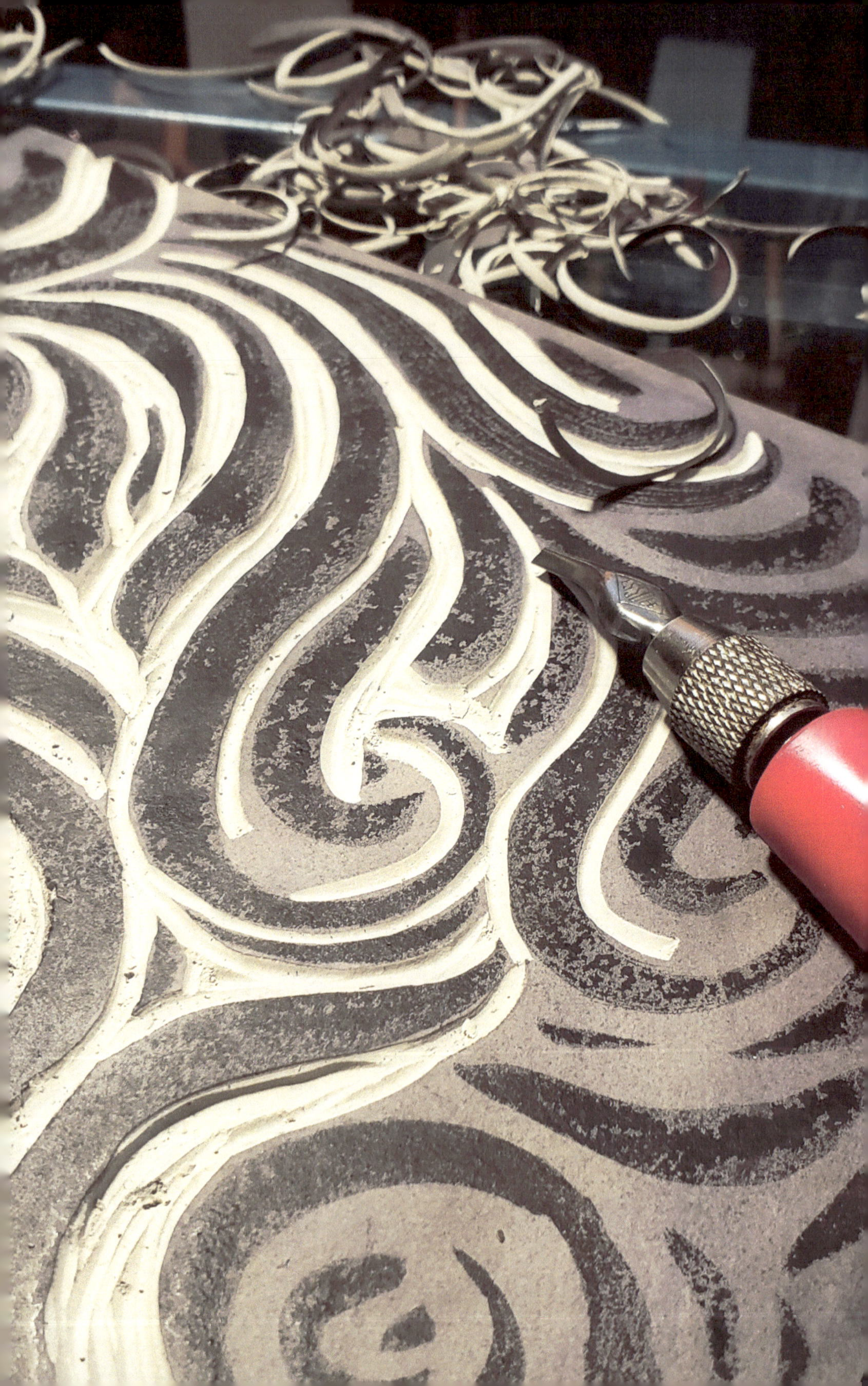

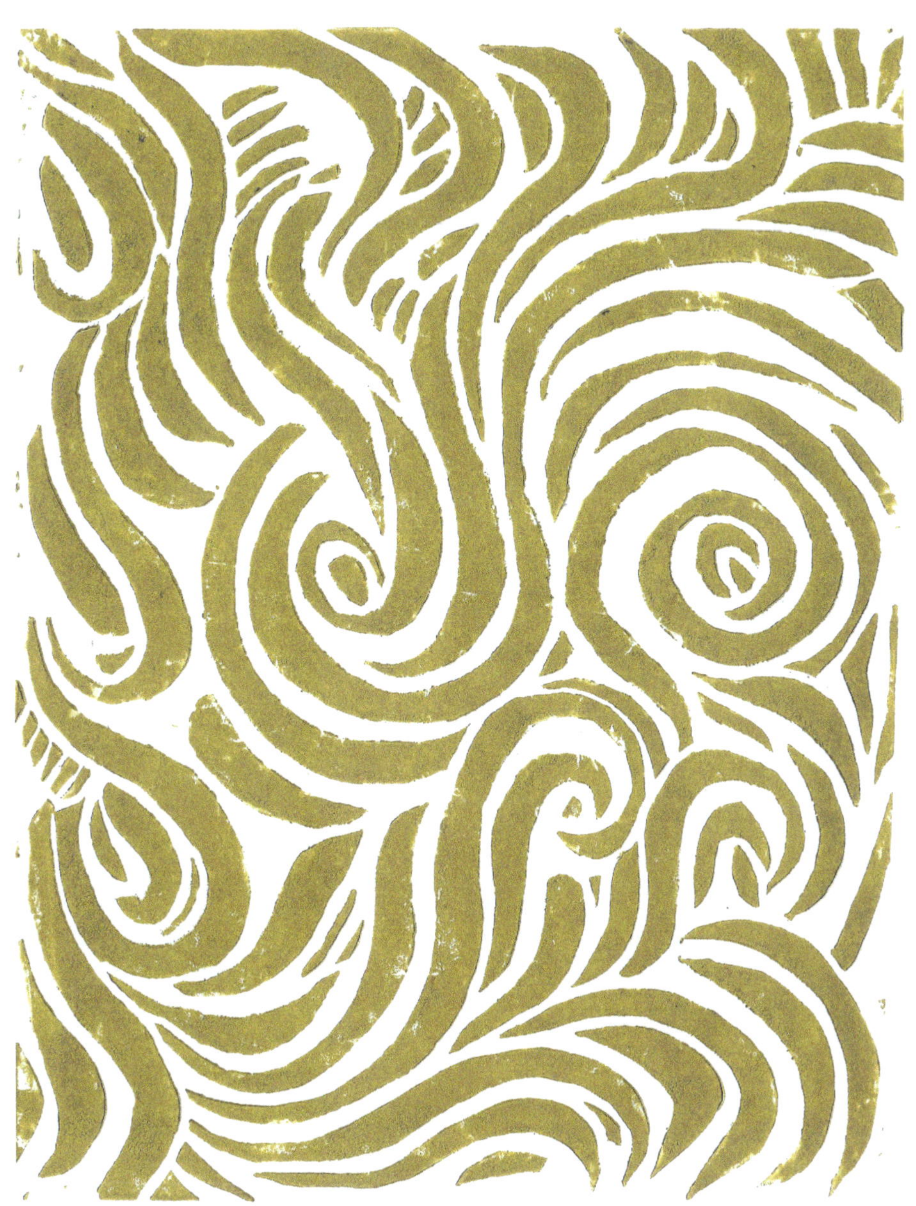

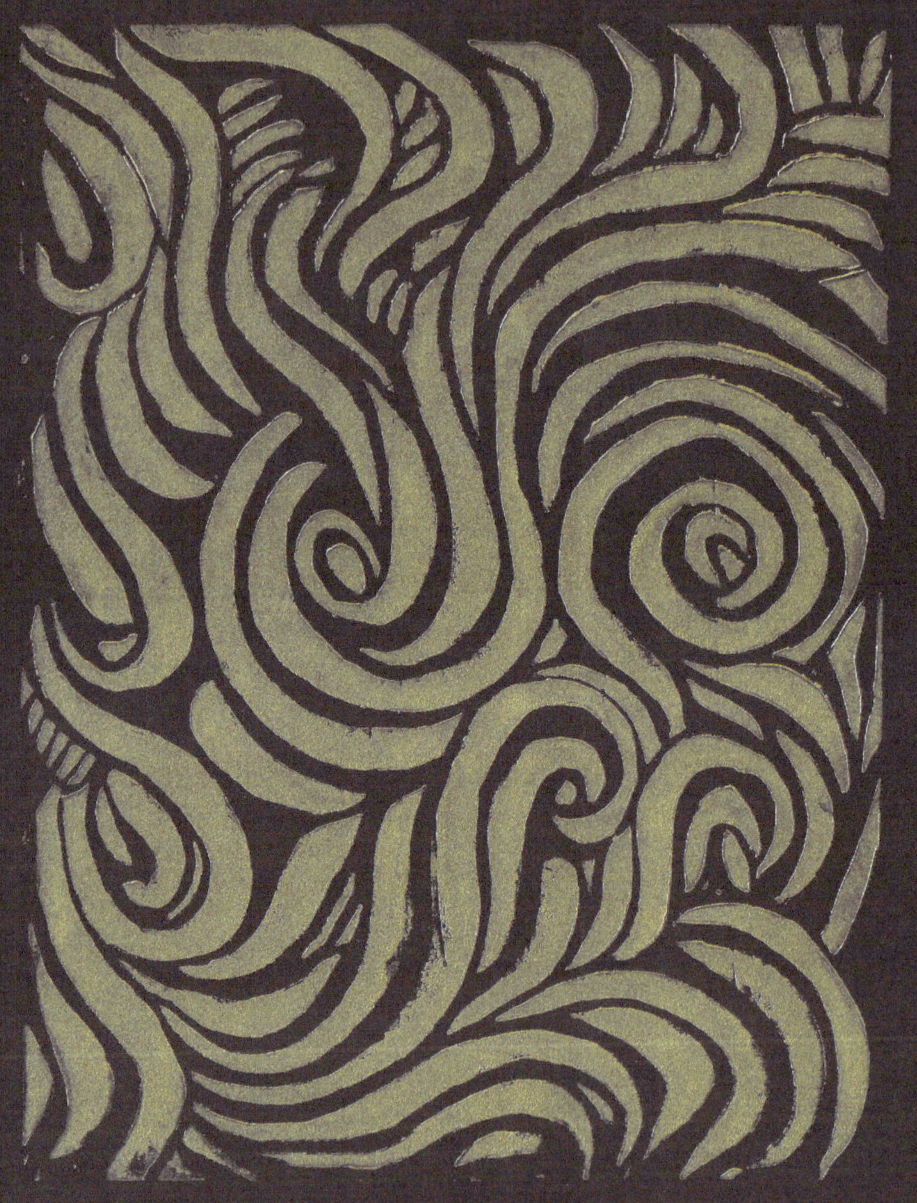

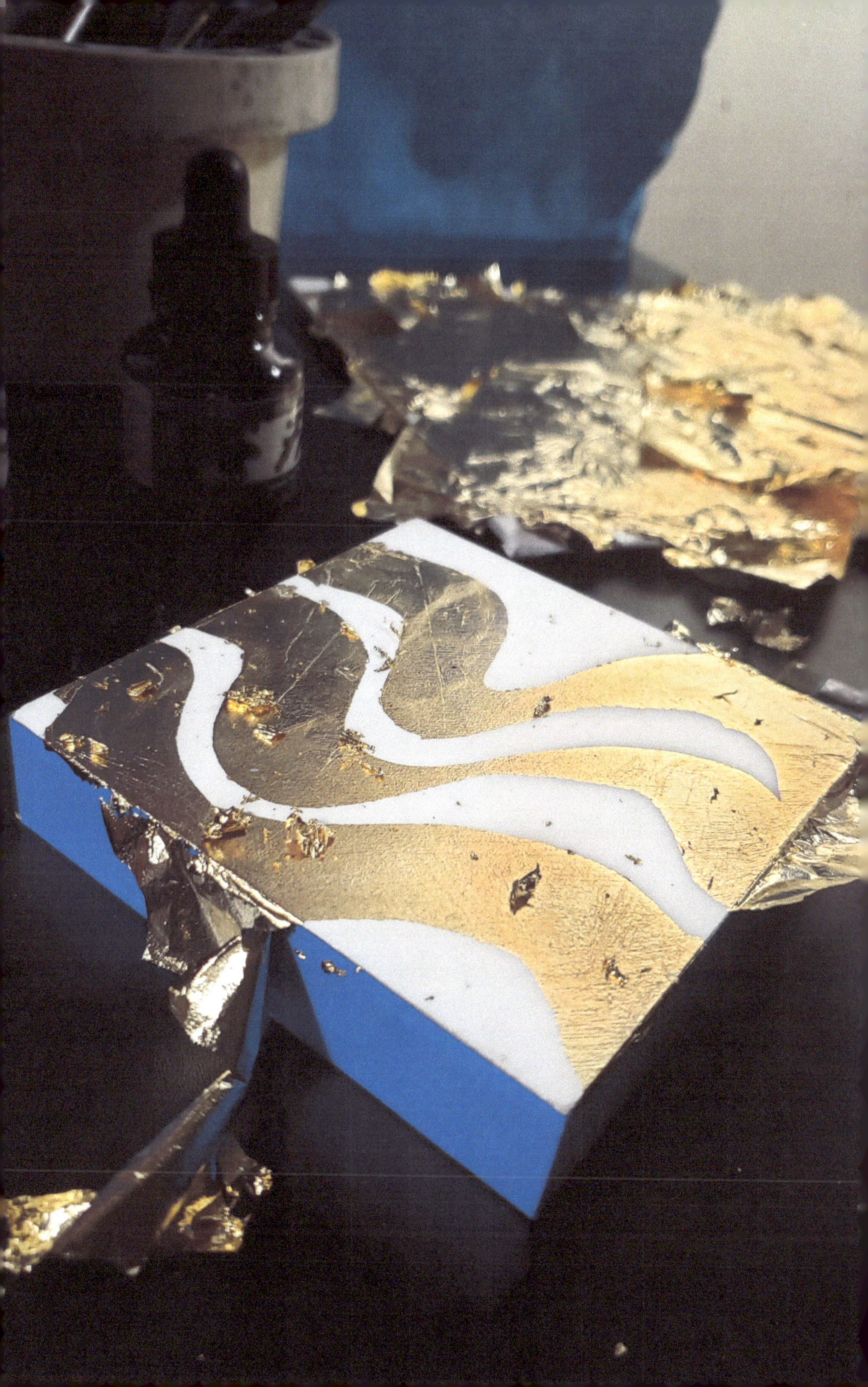

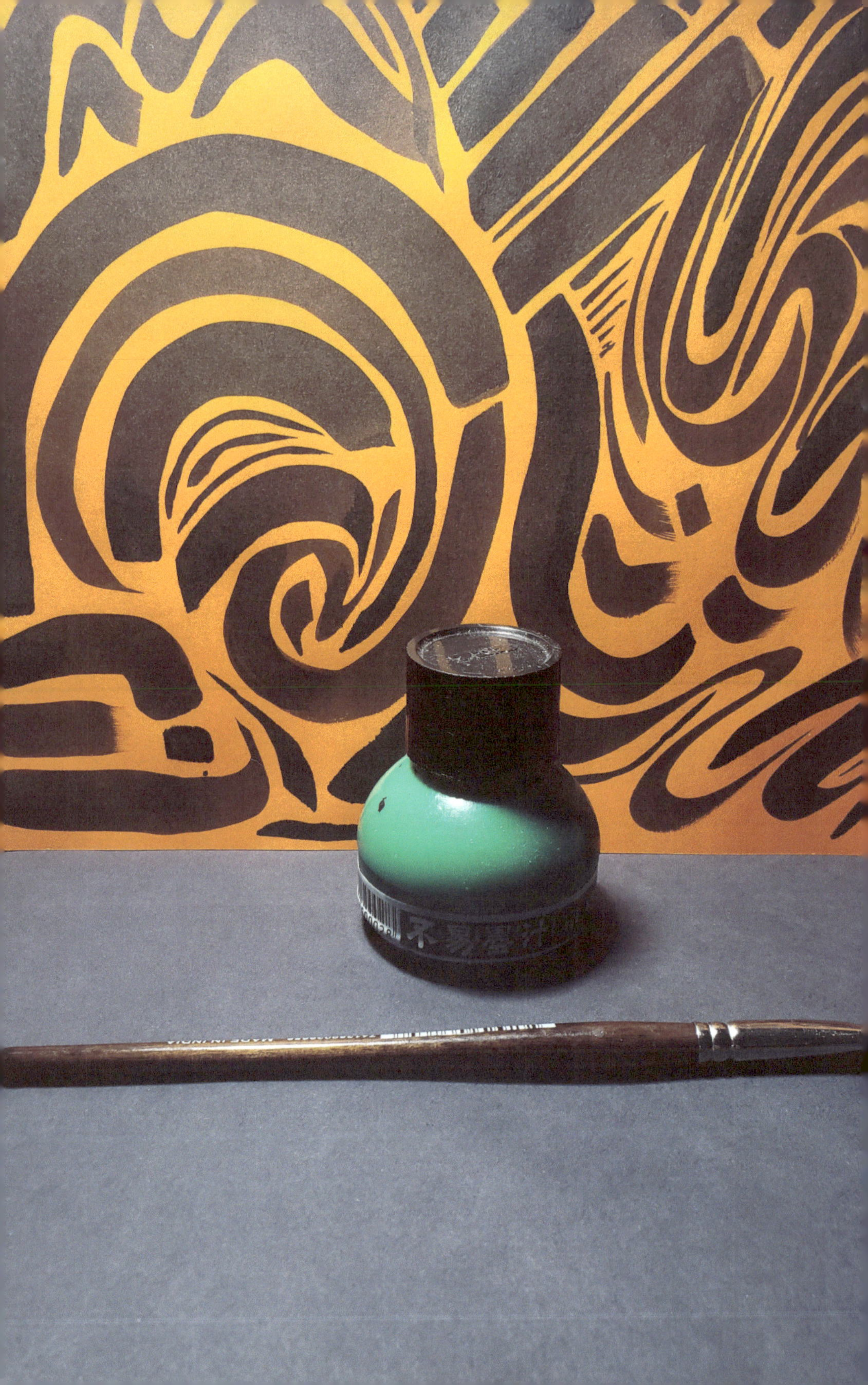
不易墨汁
MADE IN INDIA

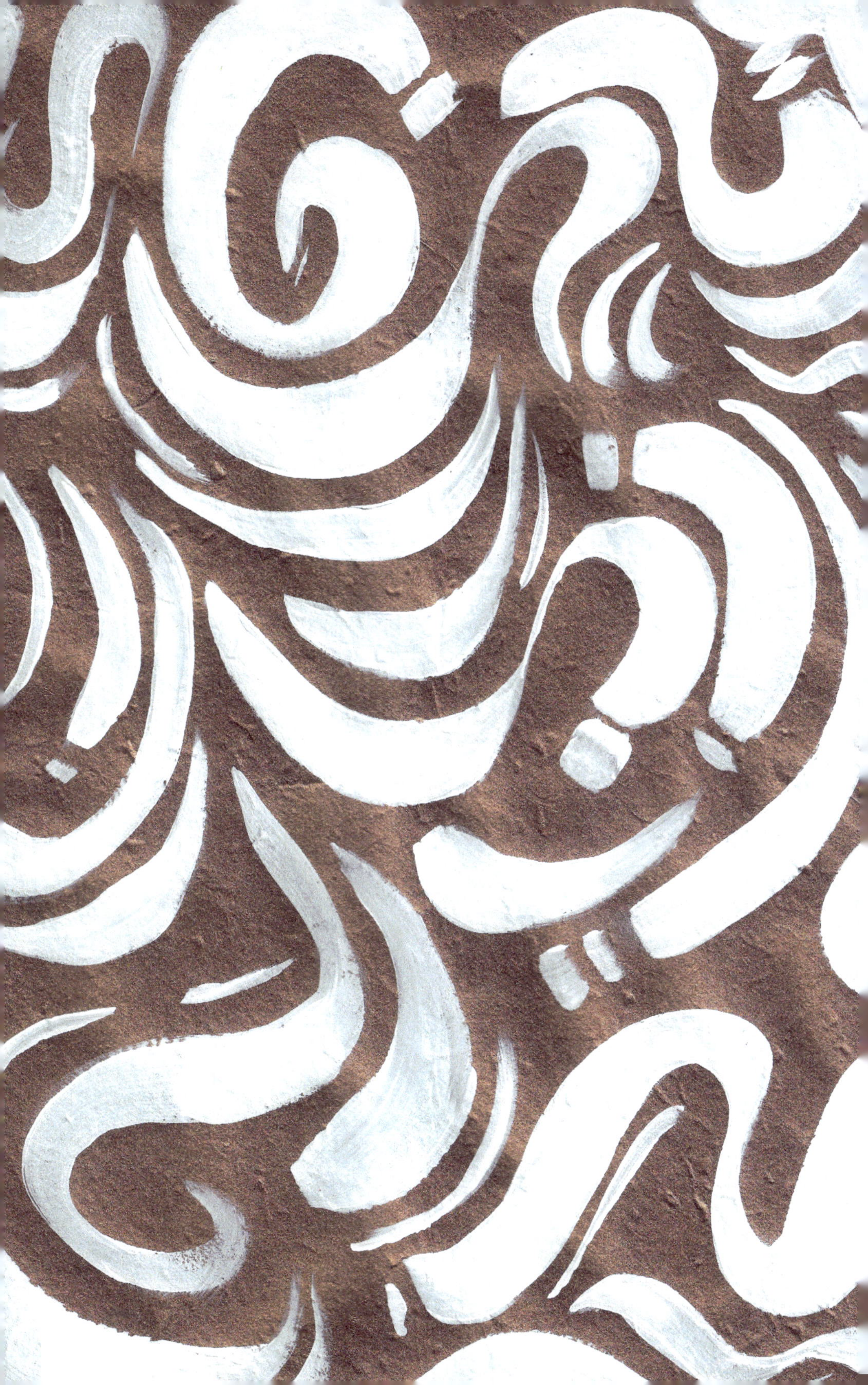

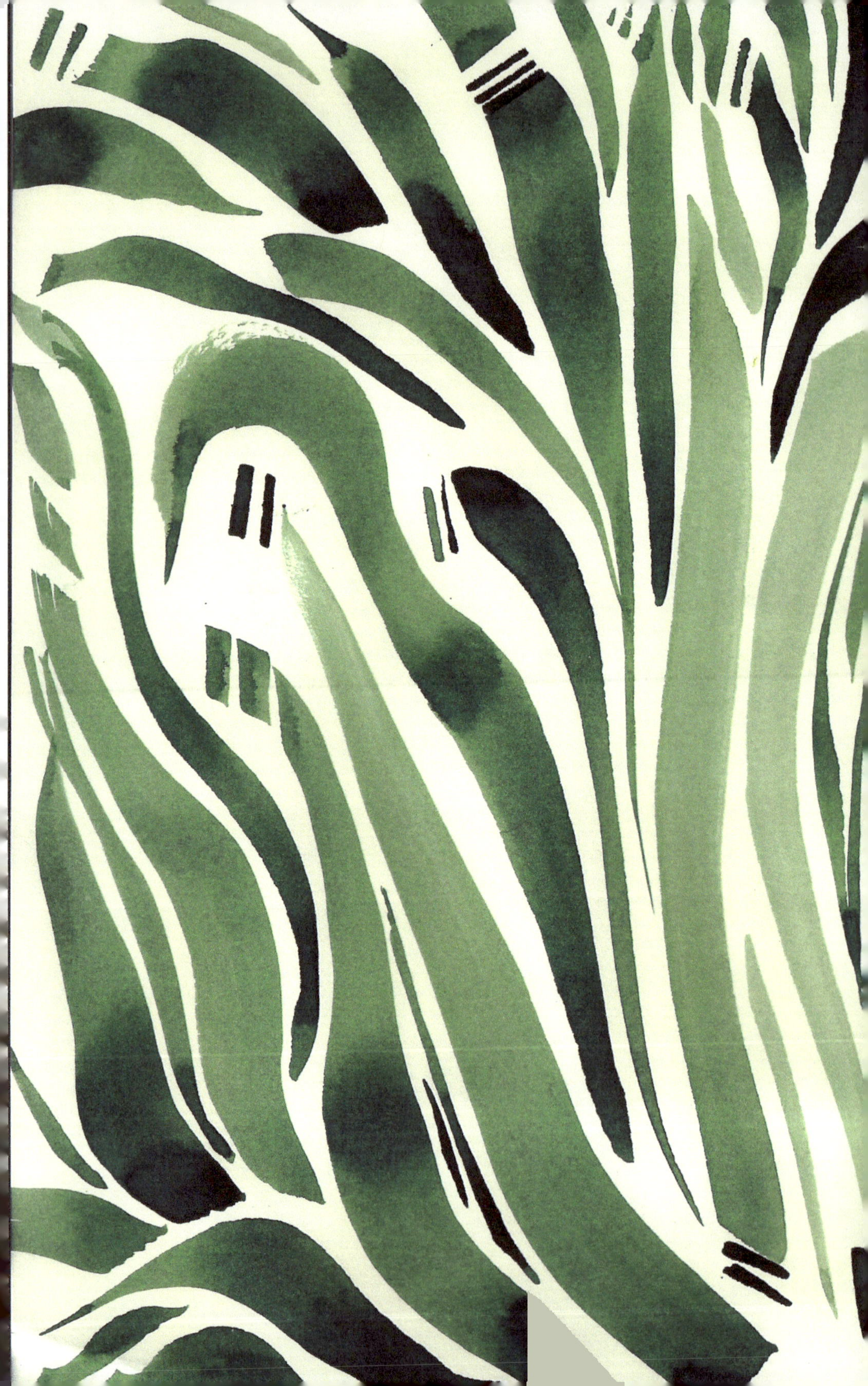

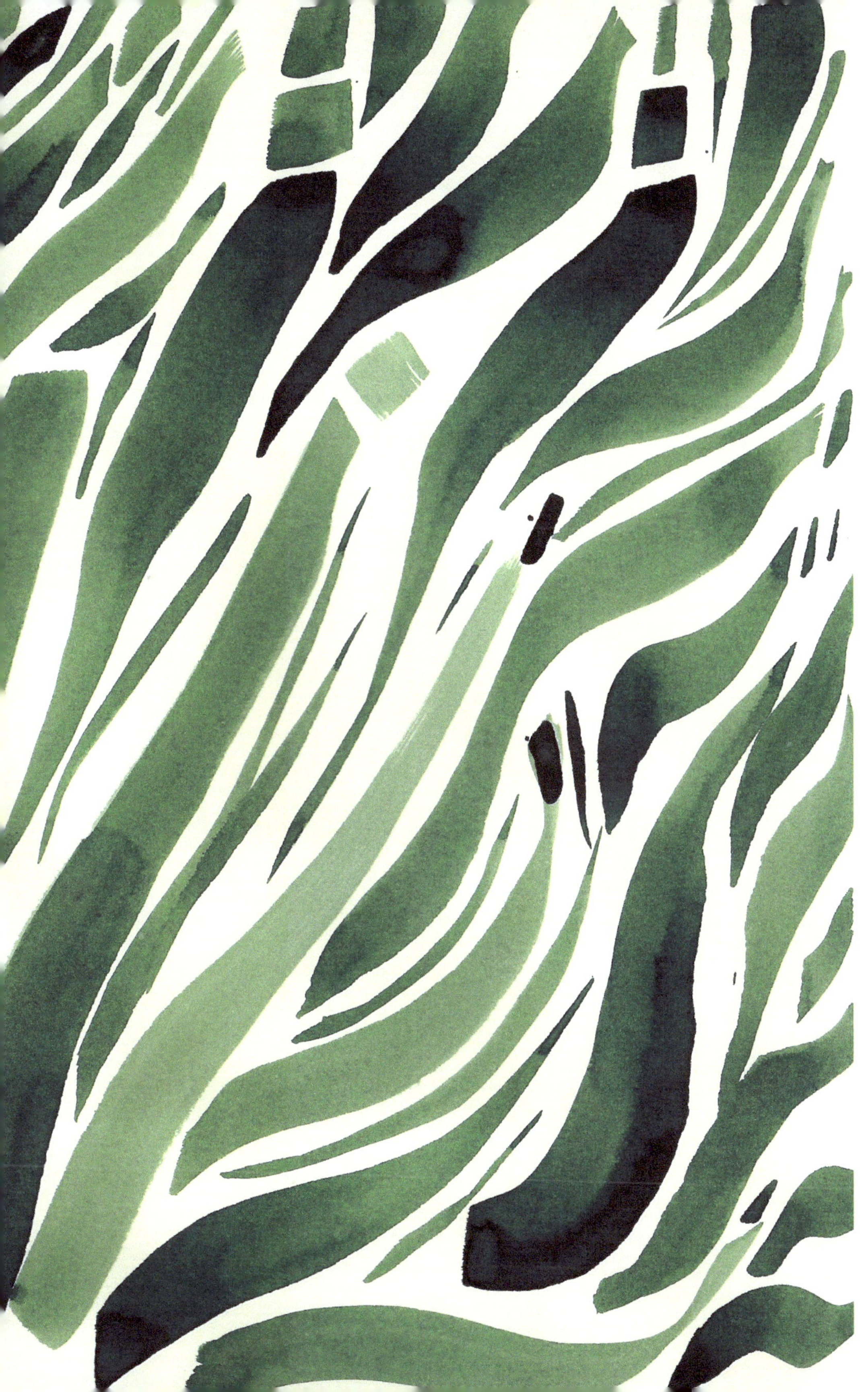

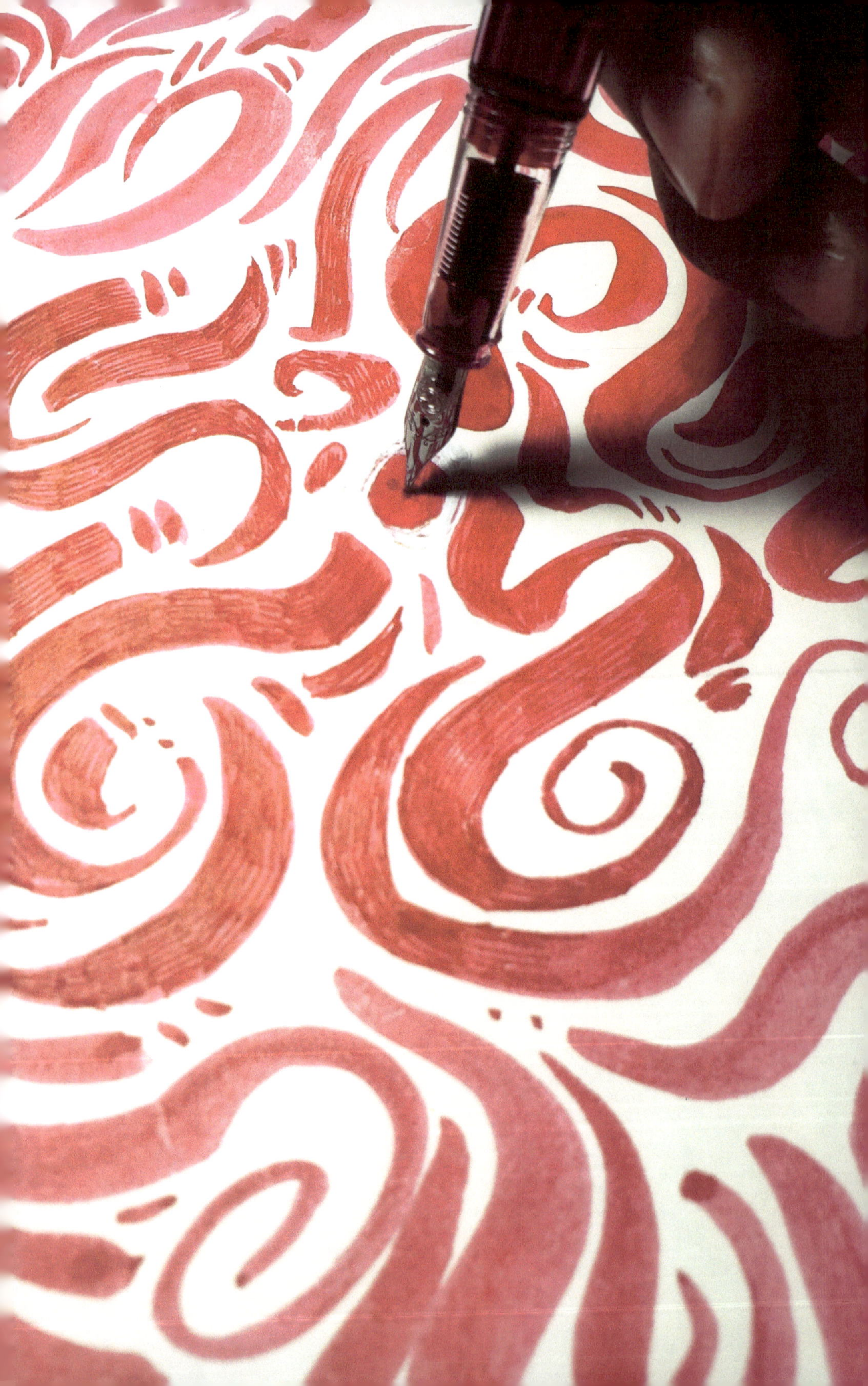

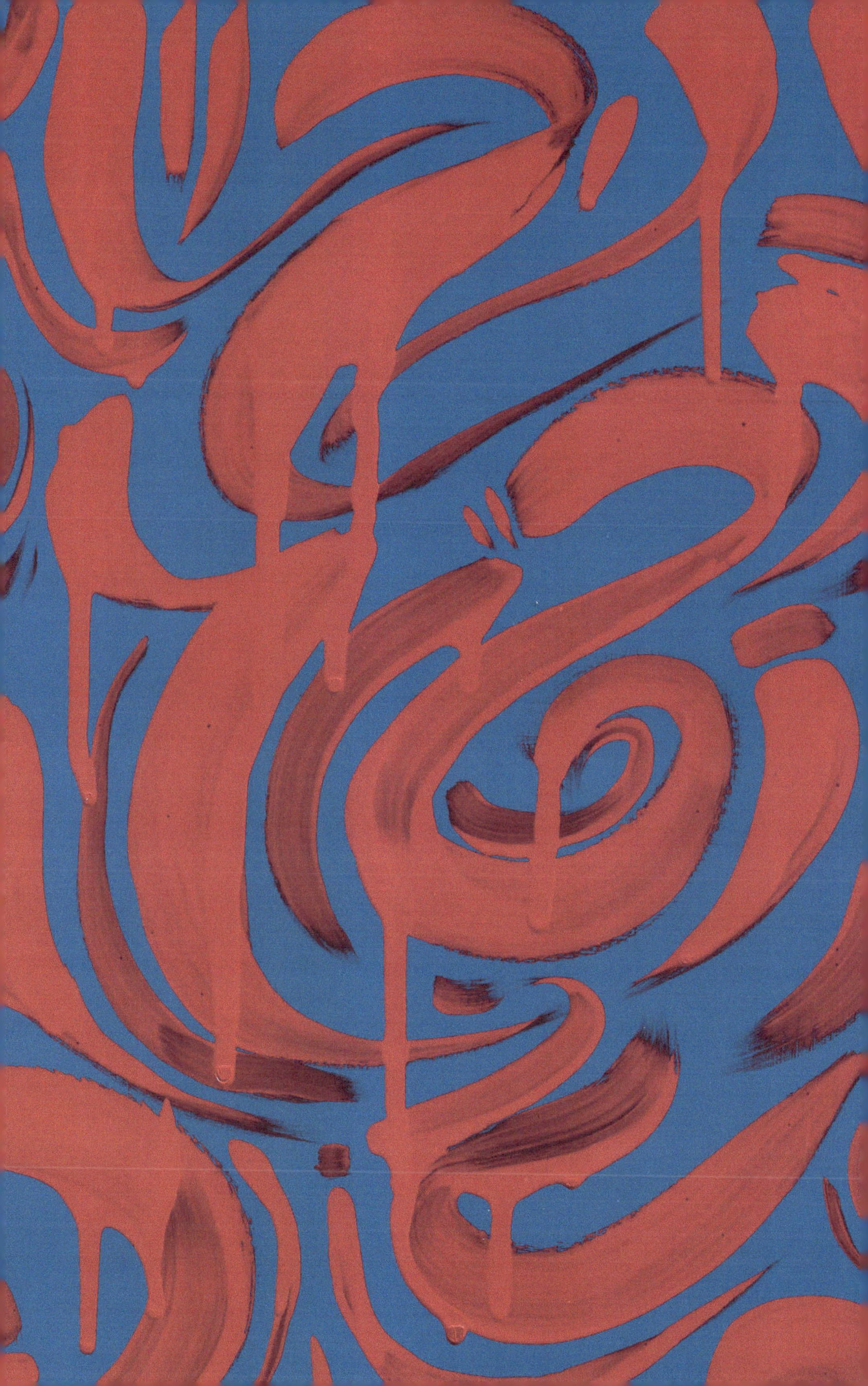

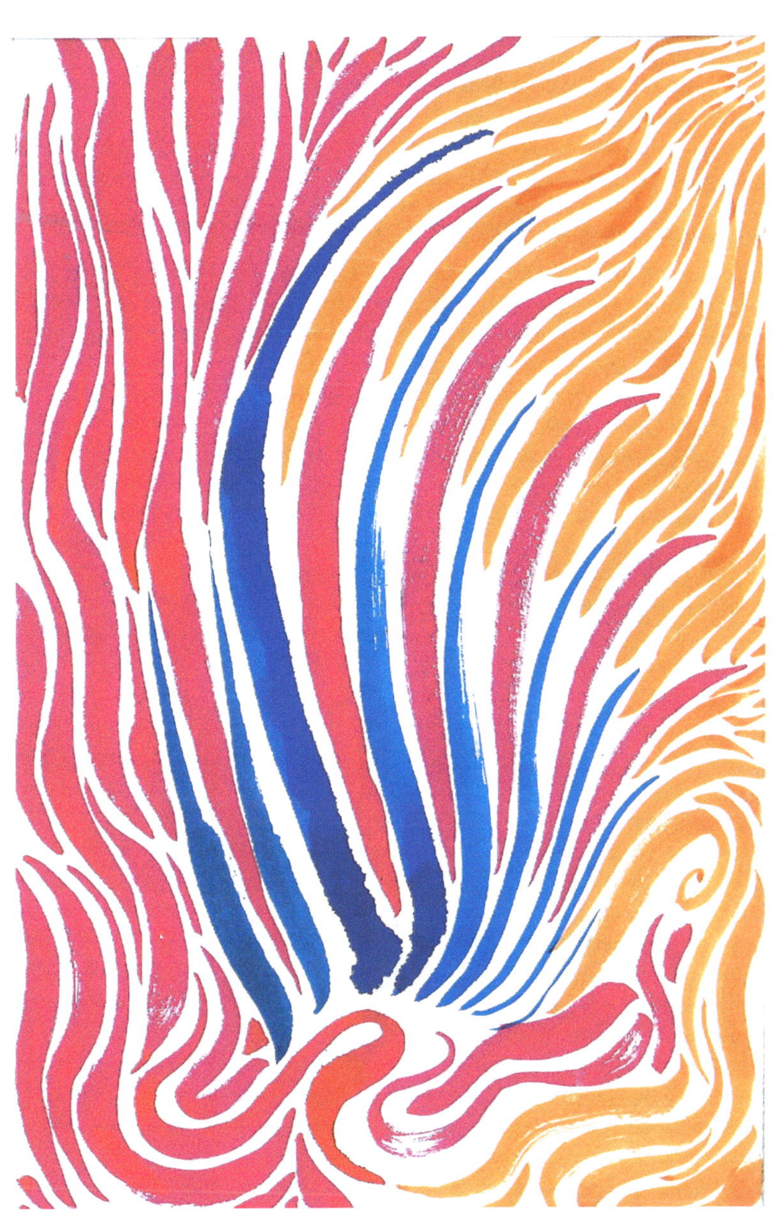

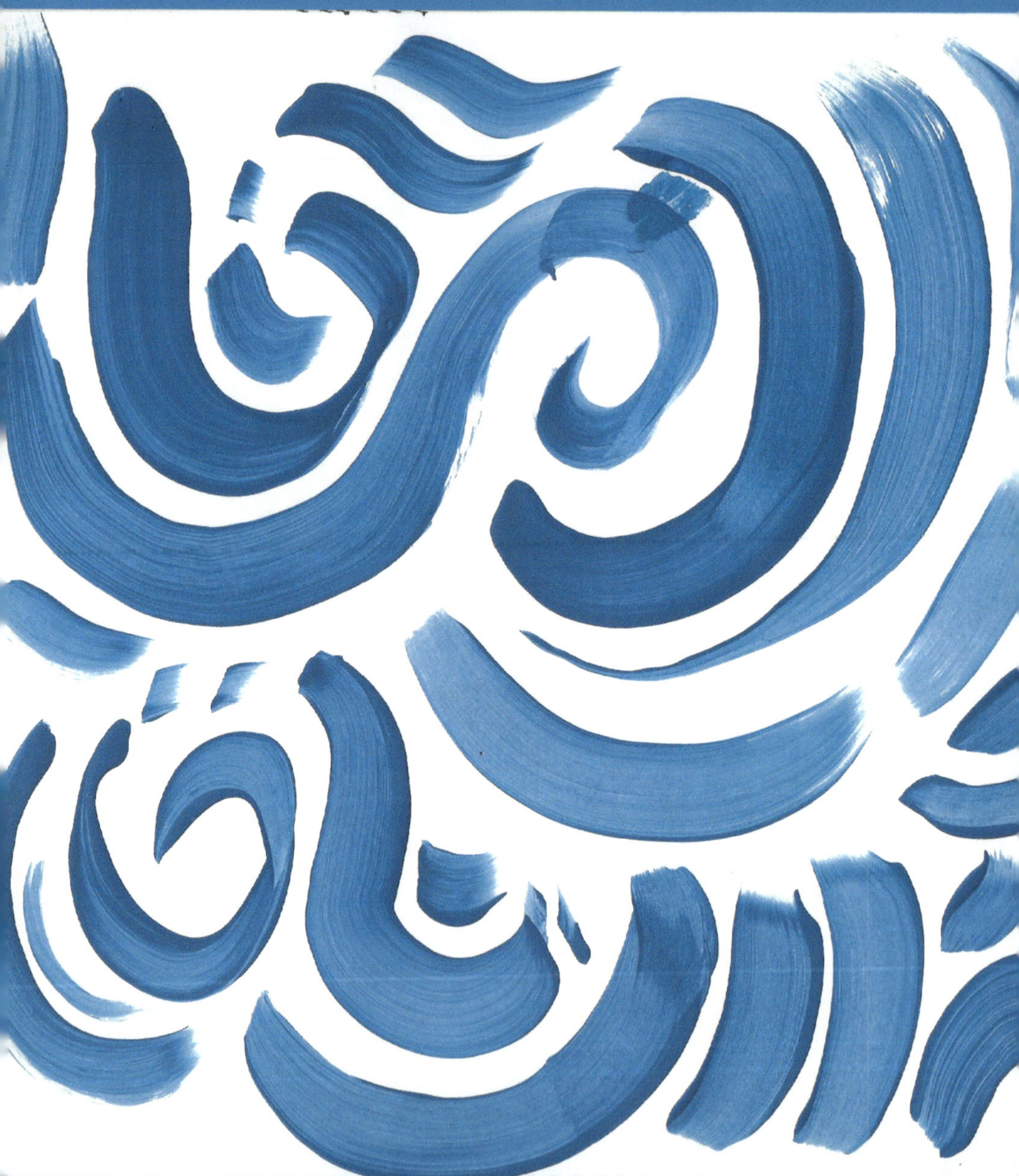

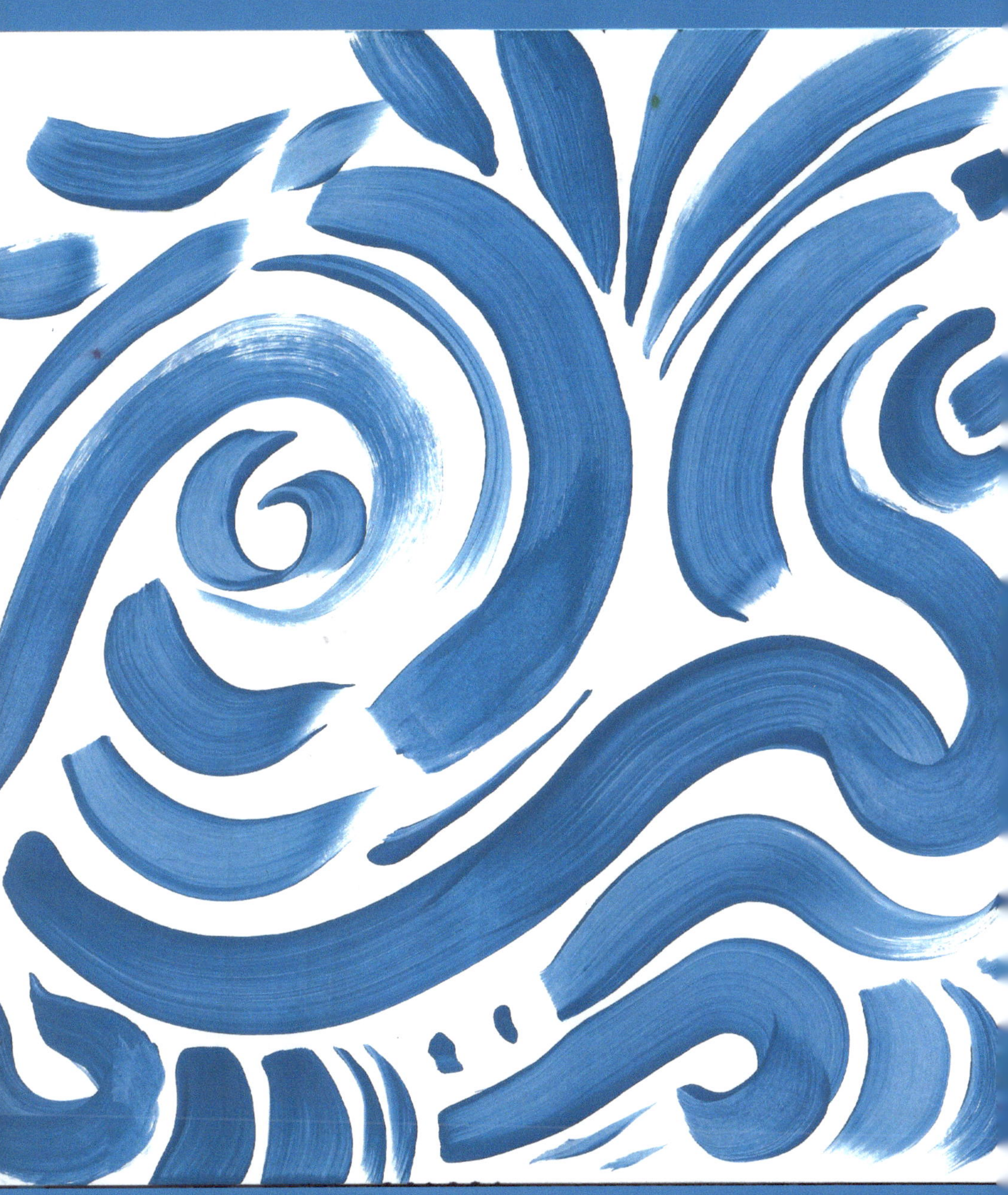

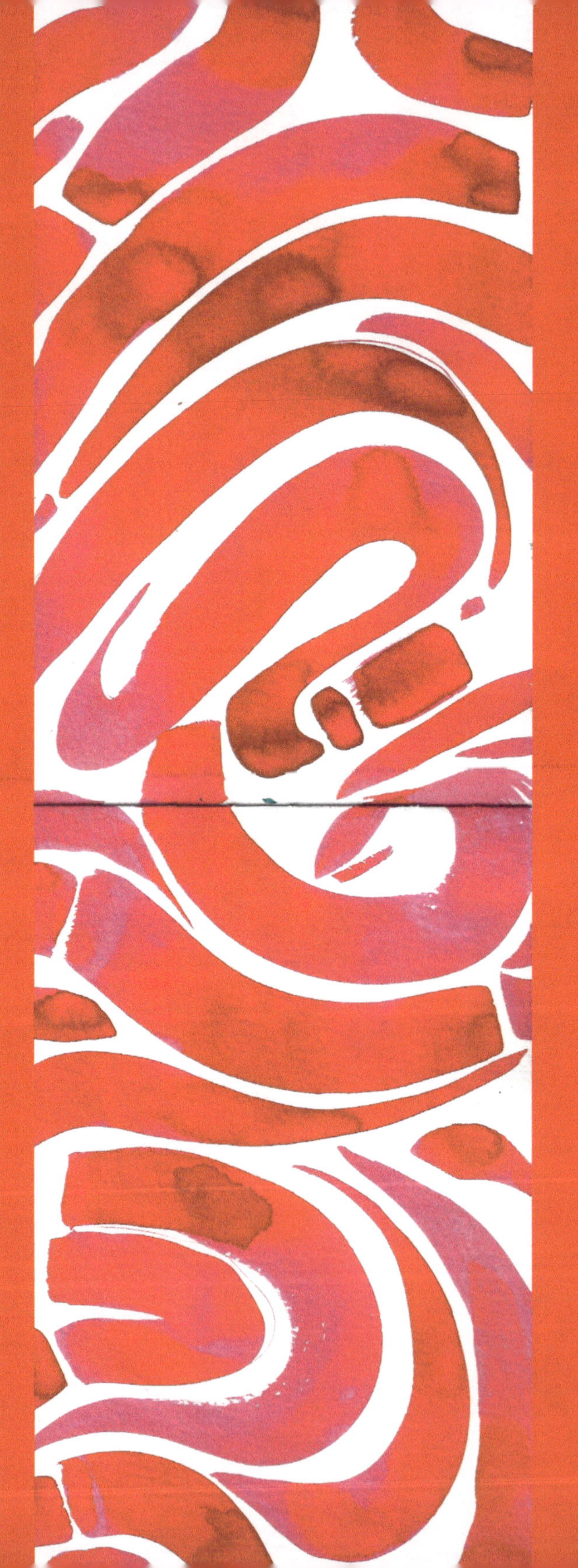

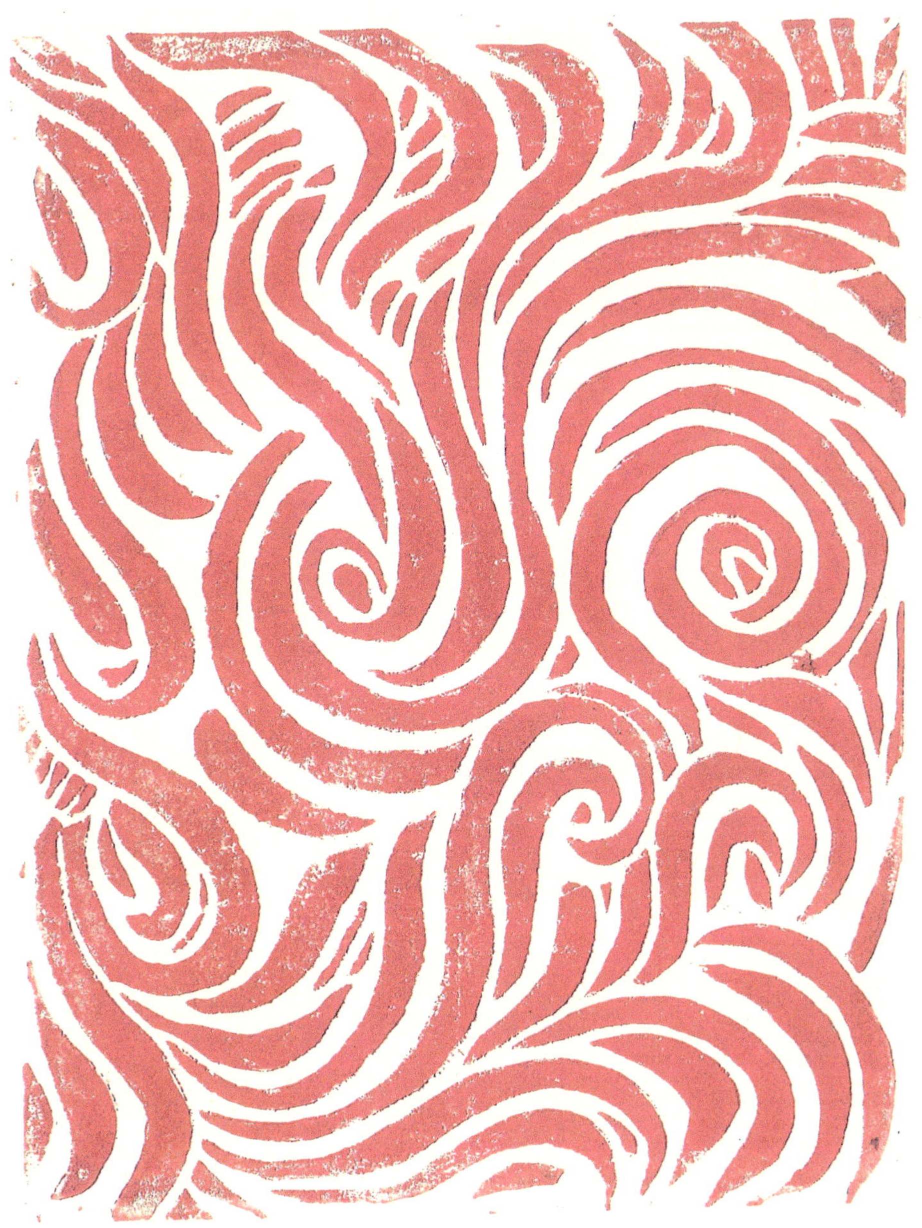

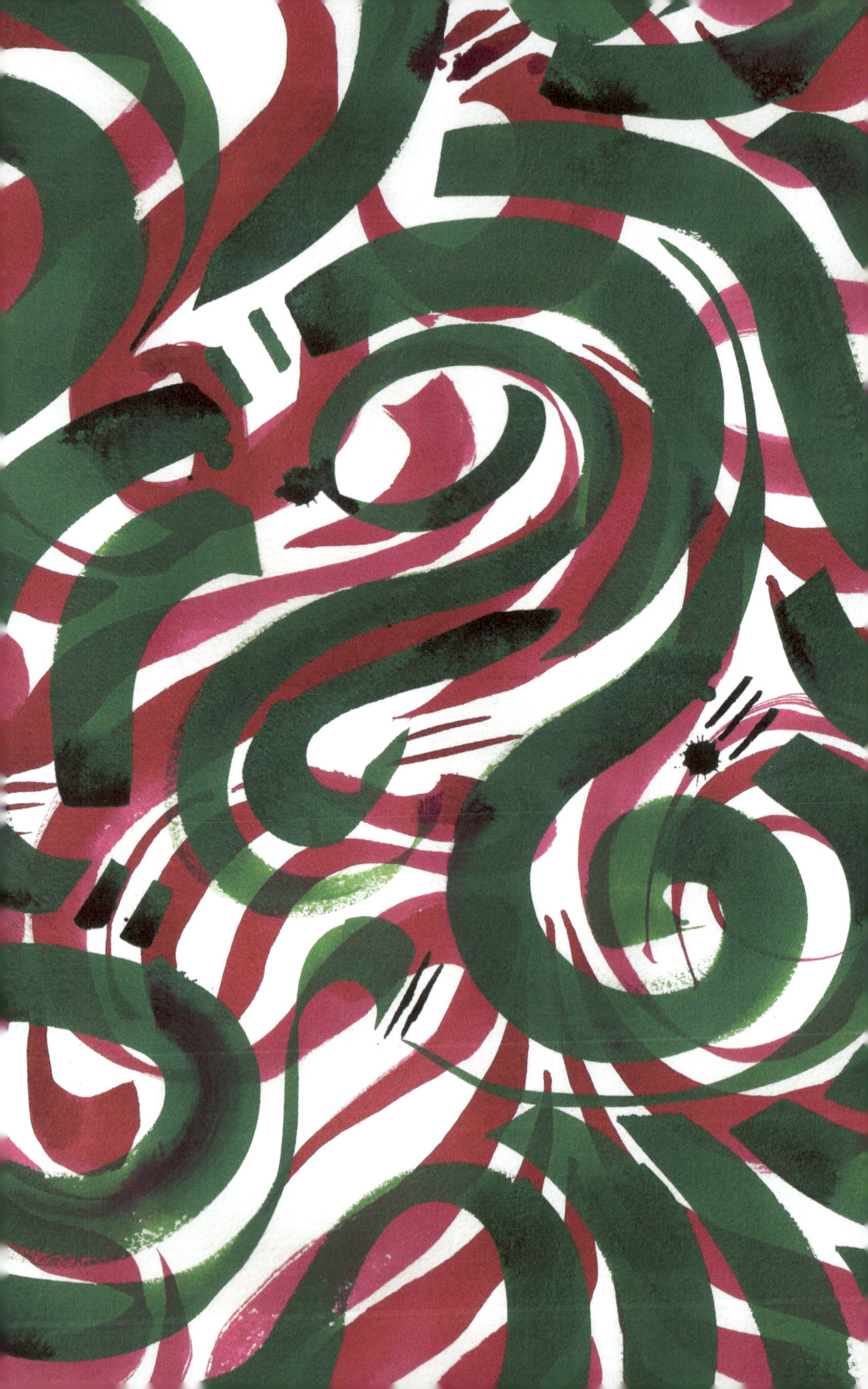

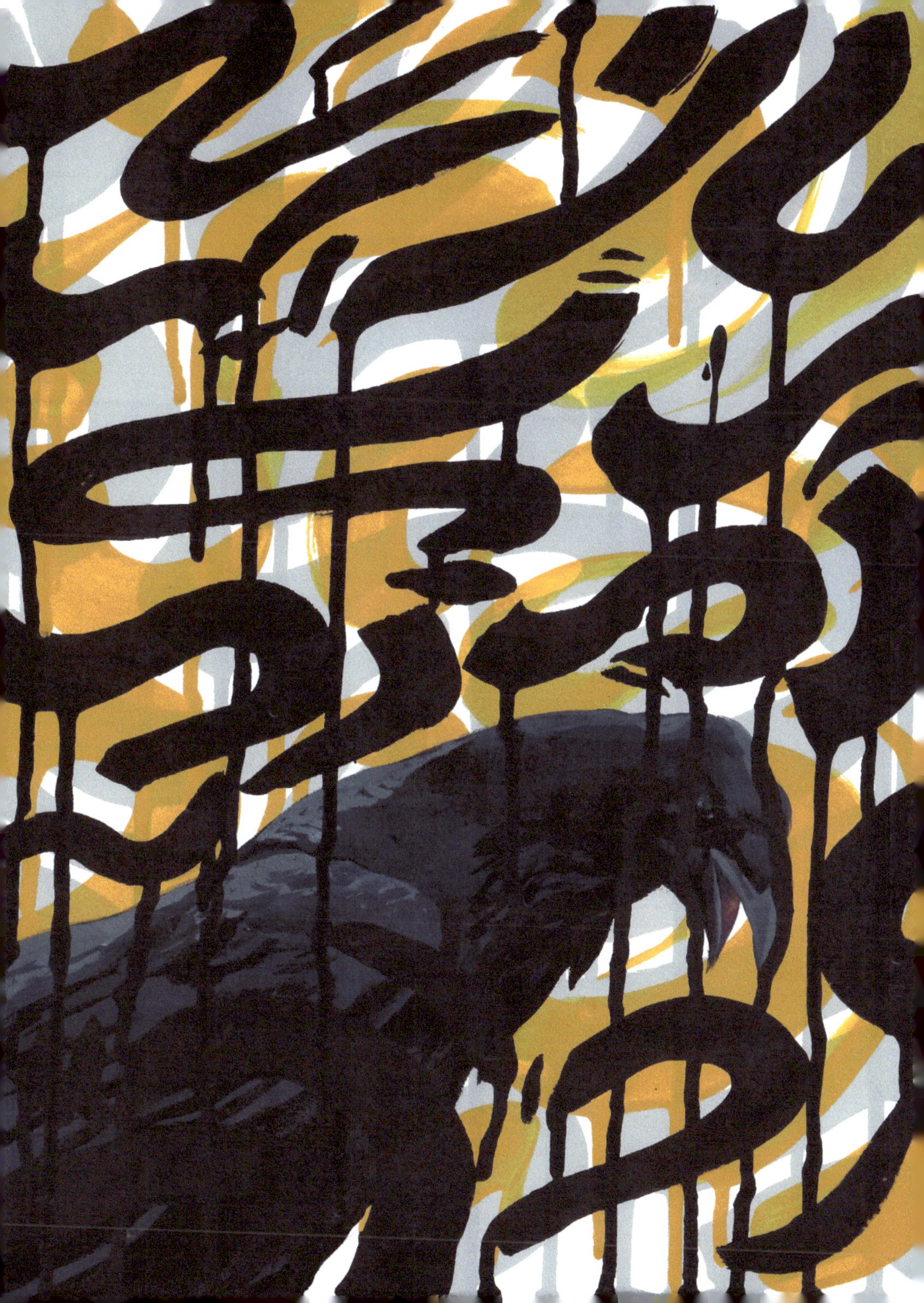

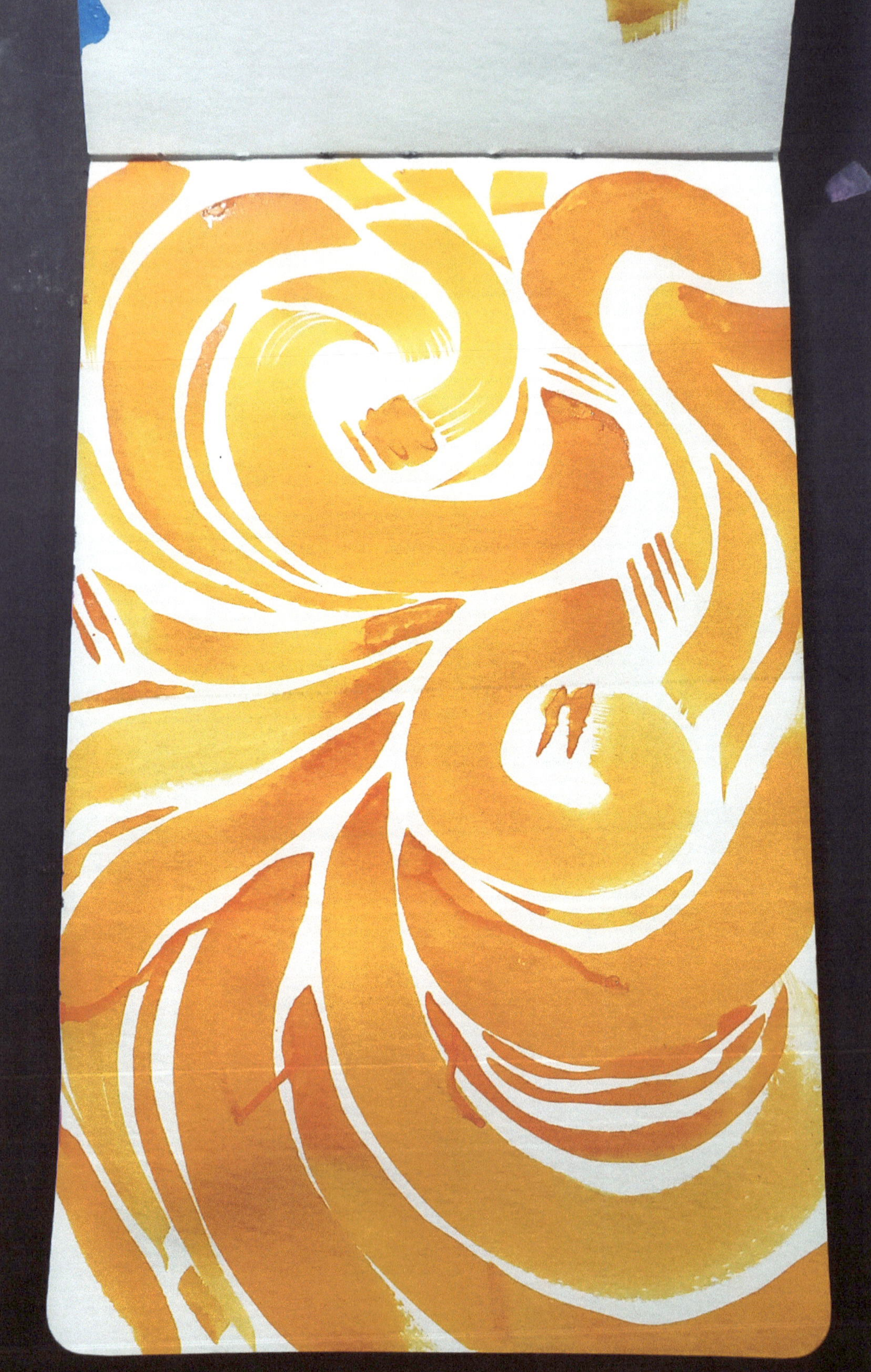

Awkward Self-portraits

As an artist I have always been uncomfortable making self-portraits. I won't speak for anyone else but for me self-portraits wither photographed or drawn force me to be face to face with my insecurities for an extended period of time. With drawing in particular I face questions like "how do I show myself the best way possible?", "Should I change this little thing or that thing to make myself more attractive?" And "how much can I change before the person in the picture stops being me?"

I decided to take my self-portraits in a different direction after doing portraits for clients who wanted me to edit their imperfections. The person in the artwork I did was more attractive after complying with their requests but it wasn't the person I was drawing, it was an idealized version of that person that didn't really exist. I wanted to as a kind of rebellion emphasize the imperfections in myself like my double chin or the gap in my teeth. It was, to my surprise, relaxing.

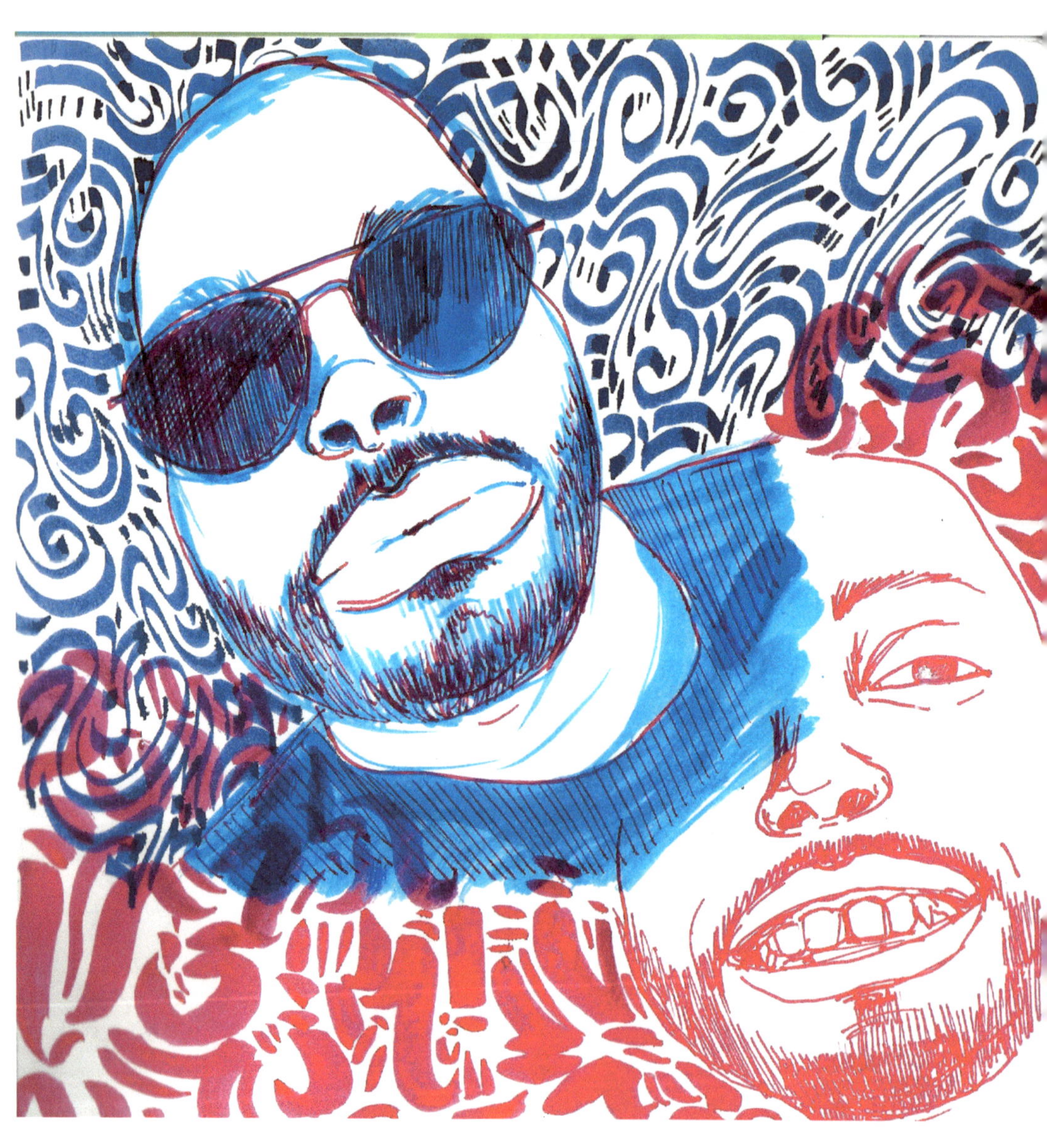

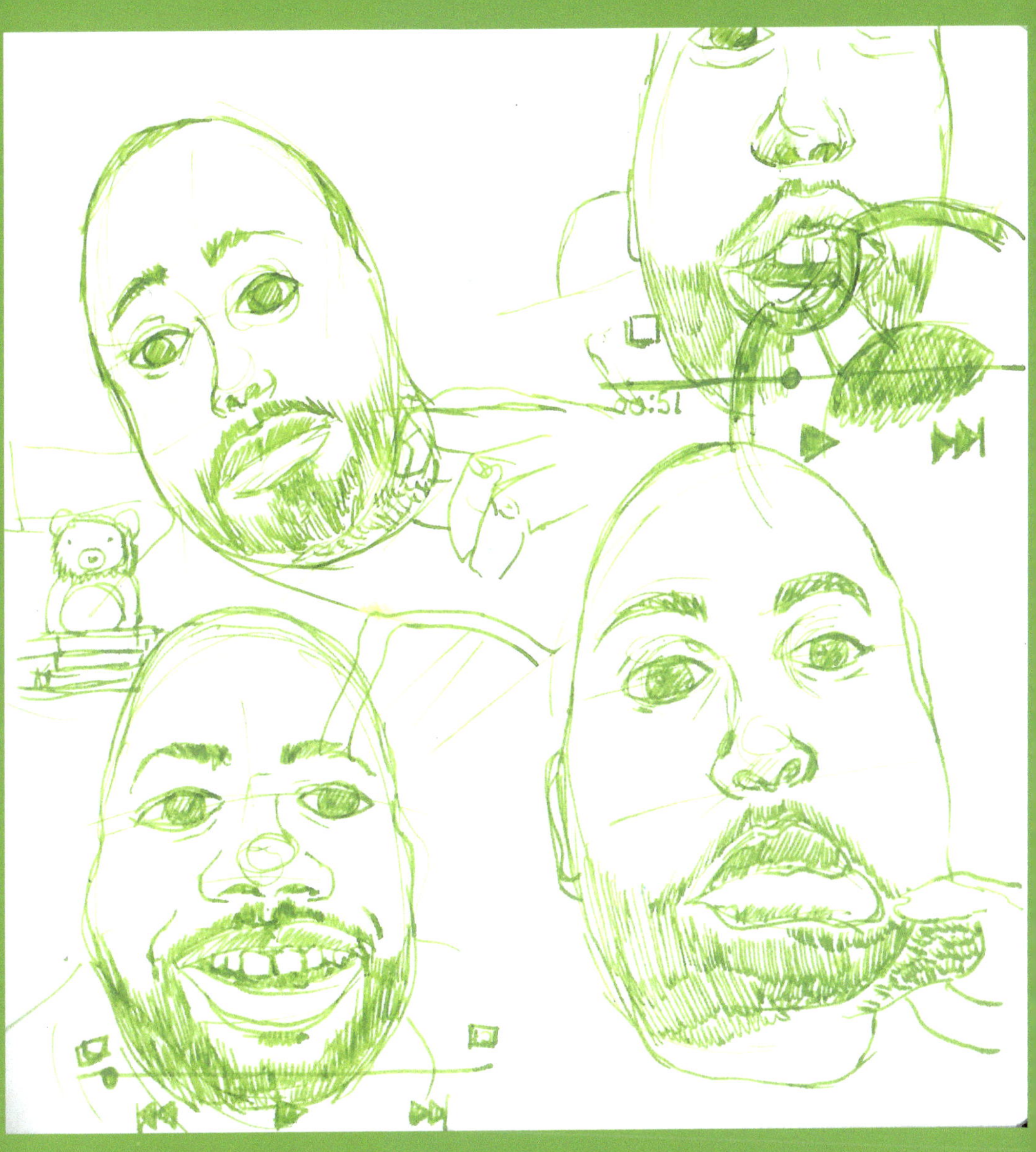

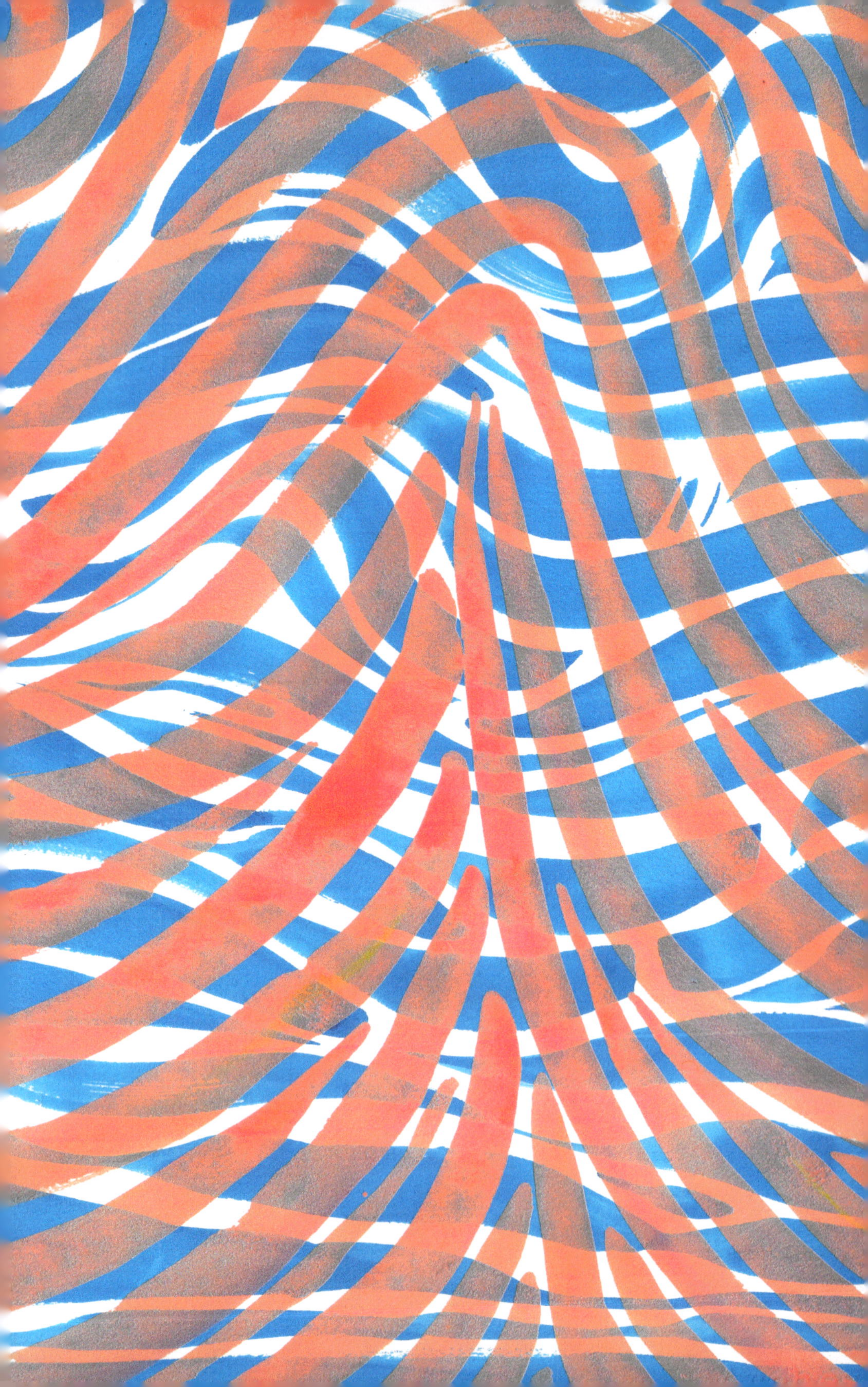

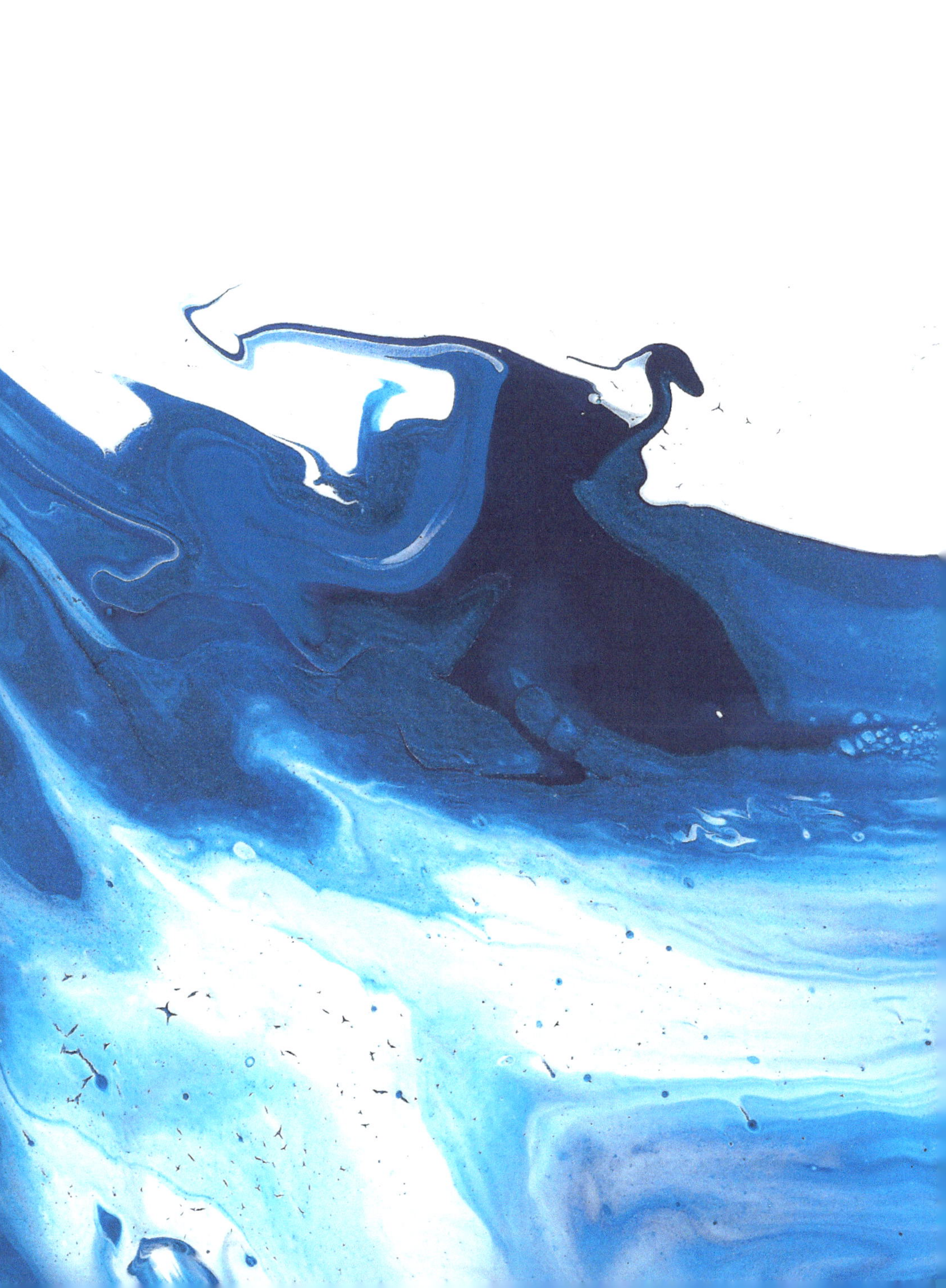

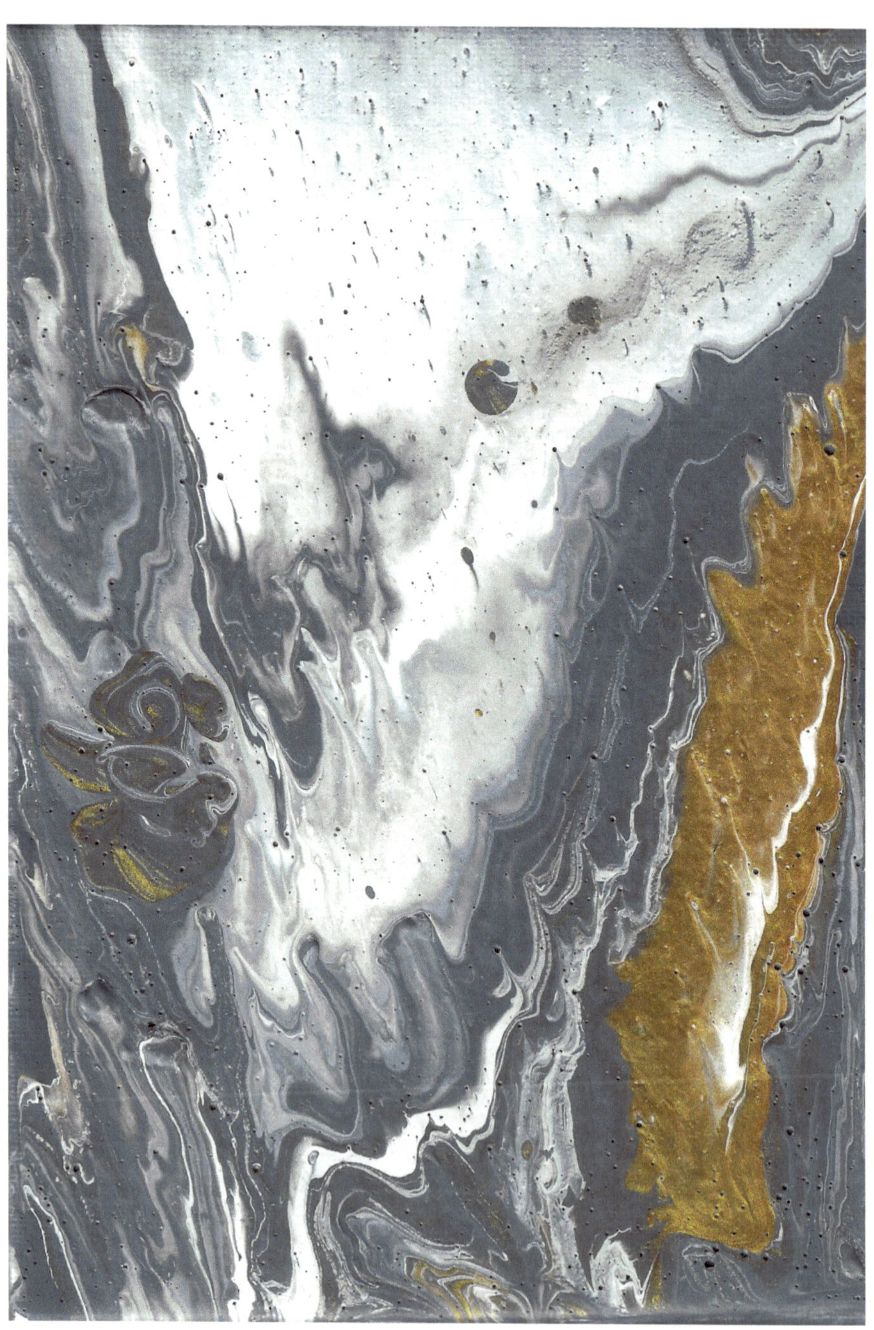

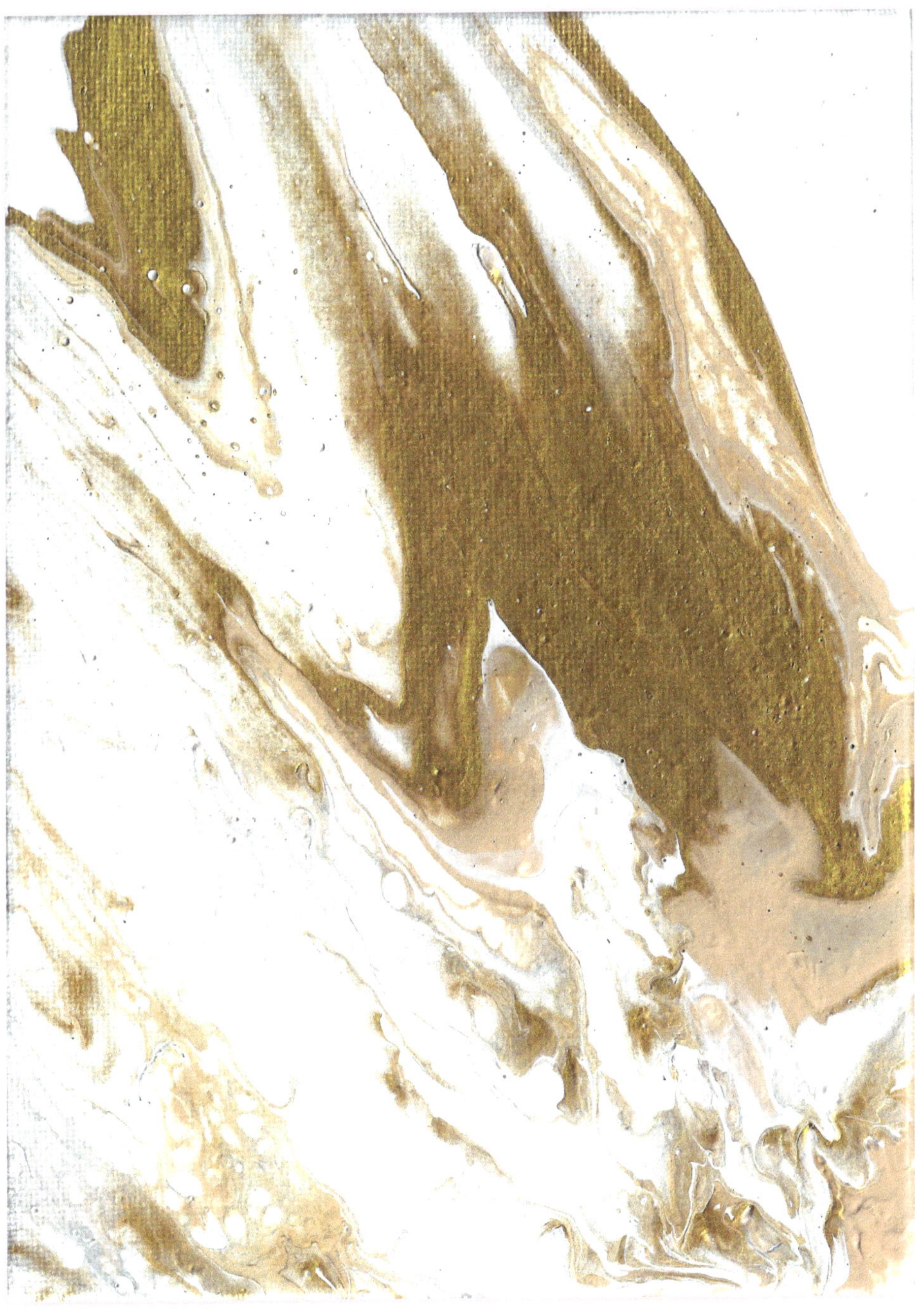

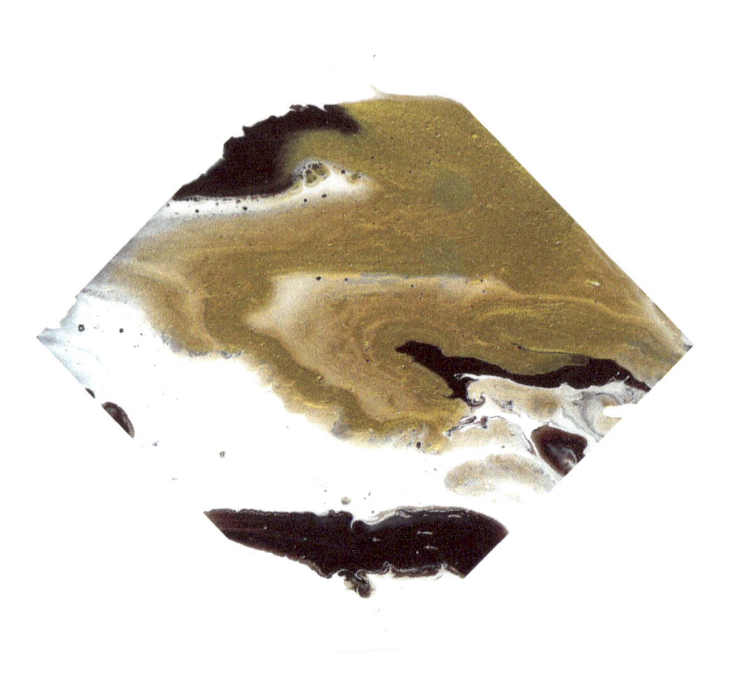

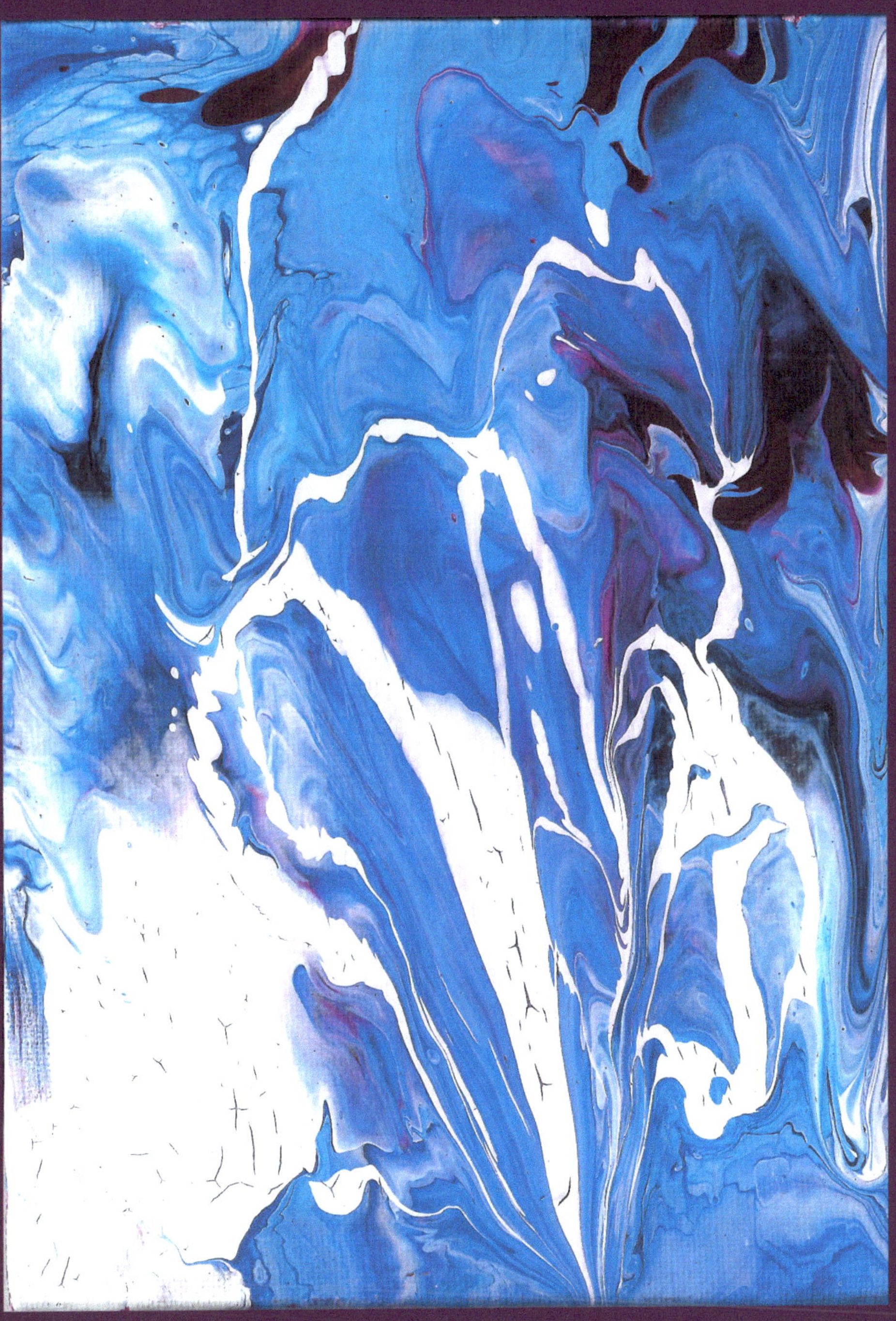

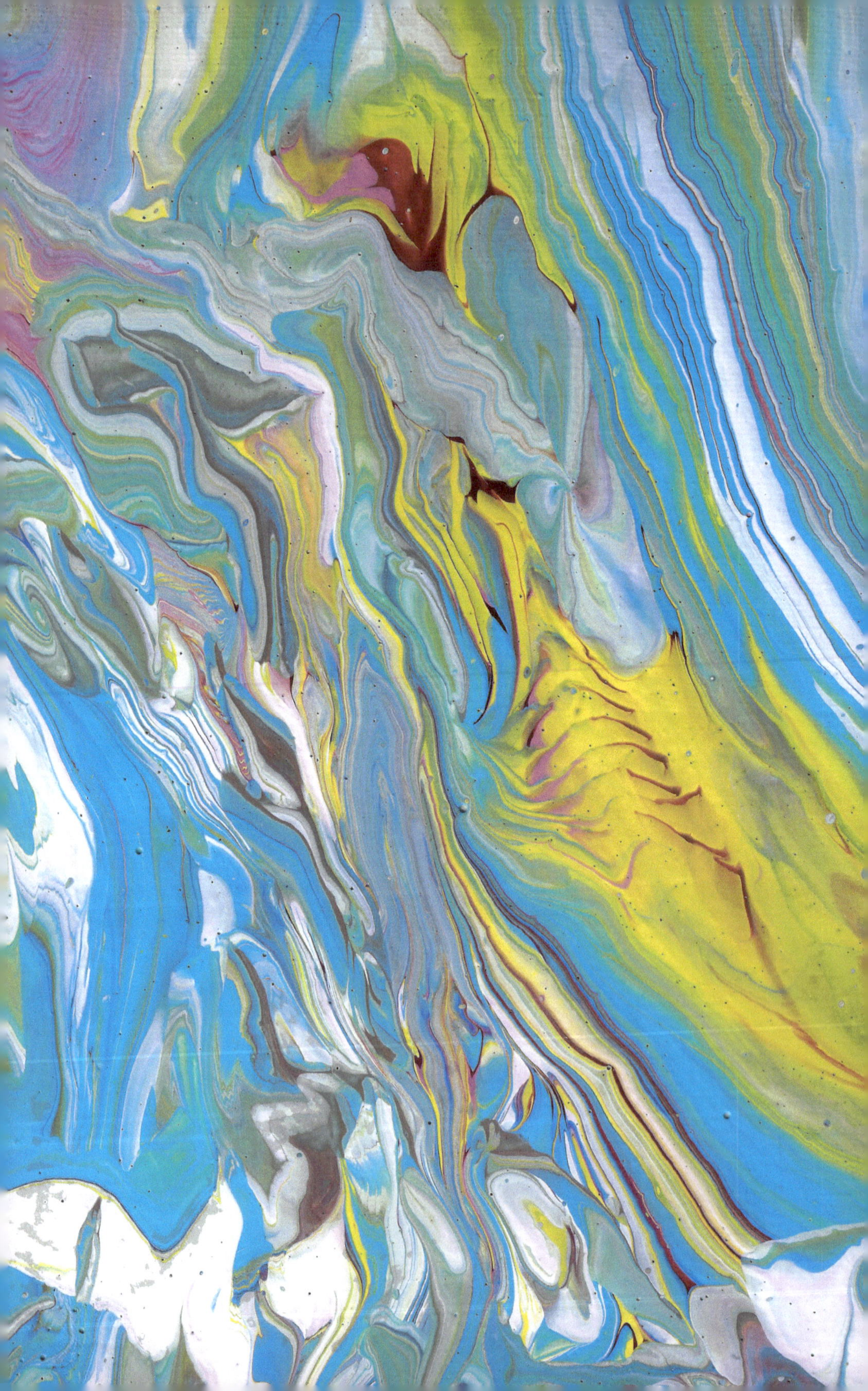

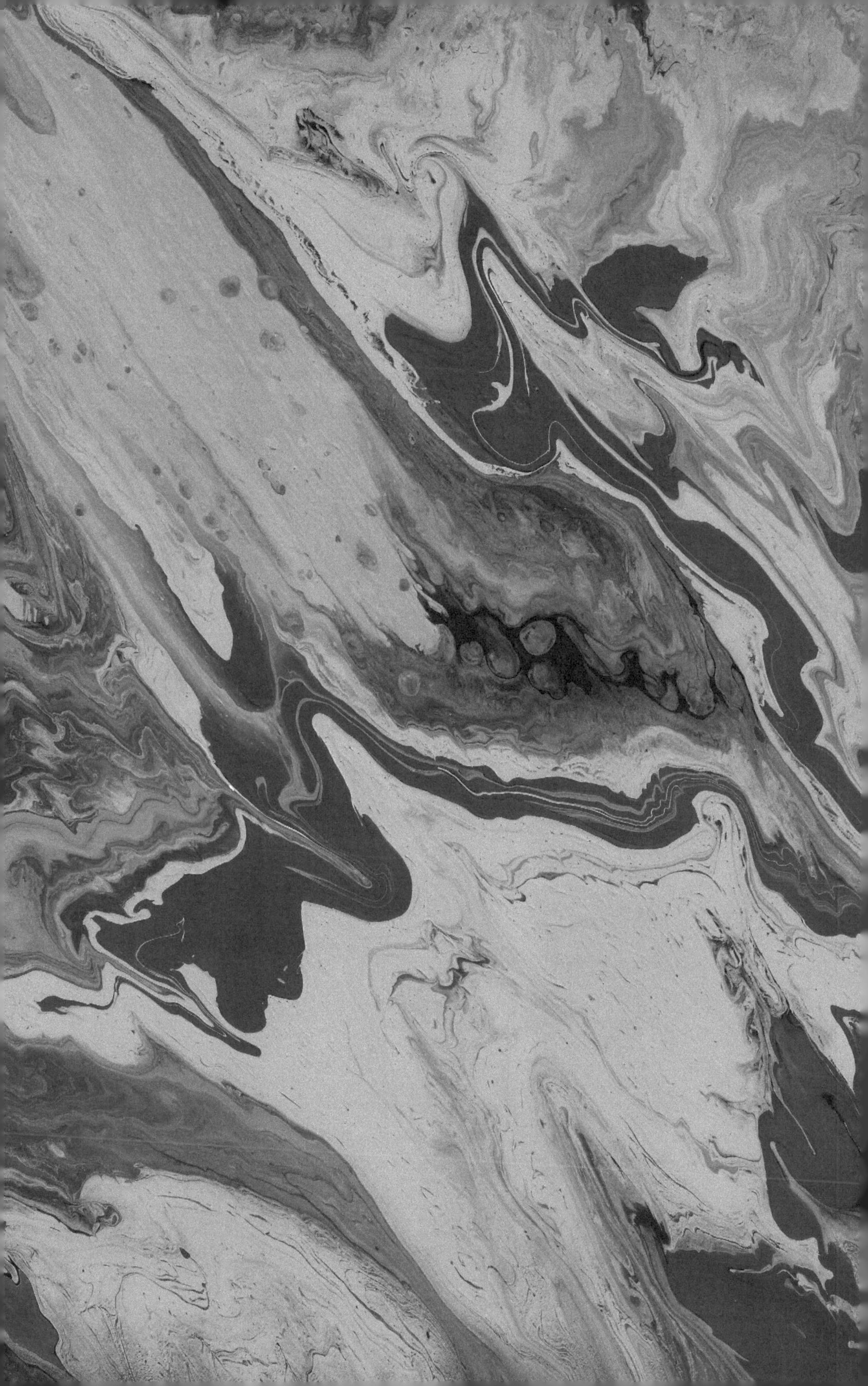

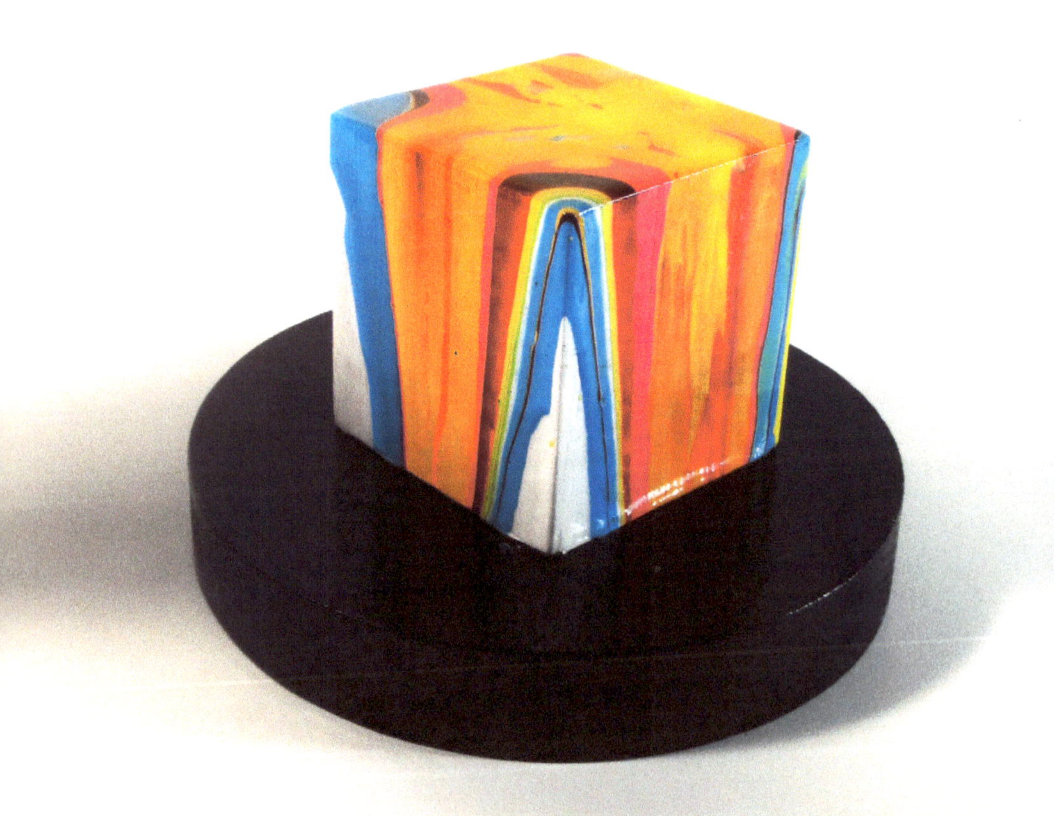

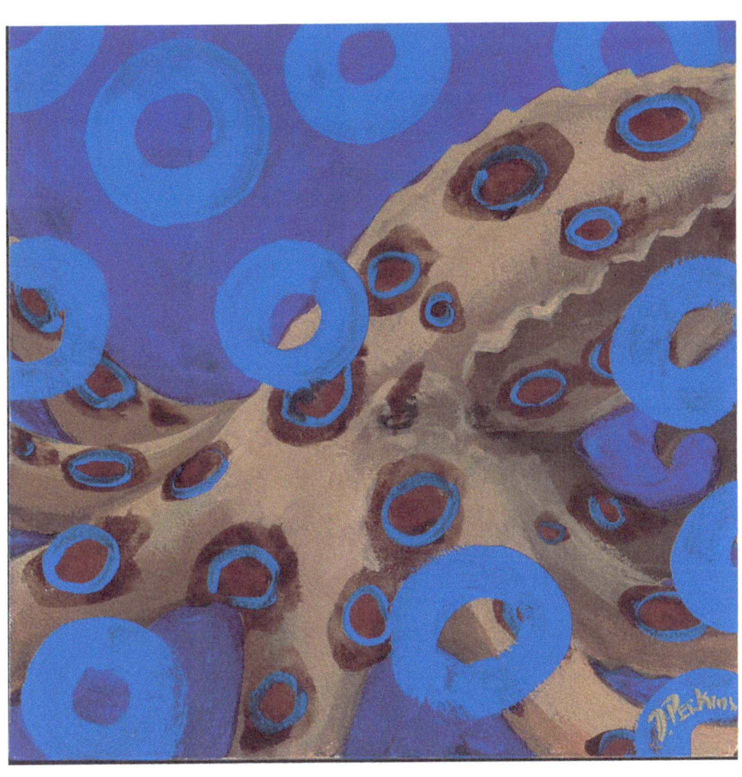

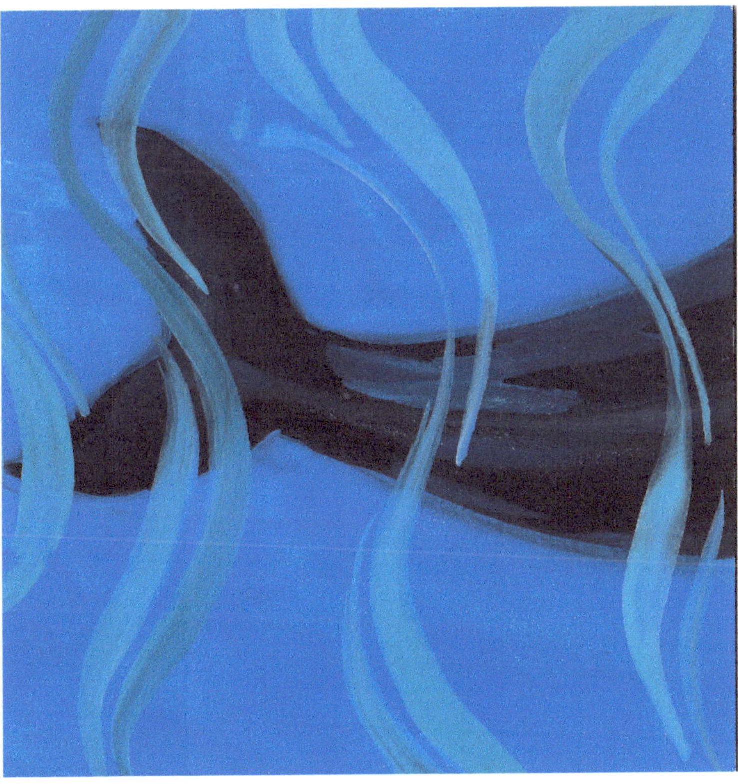

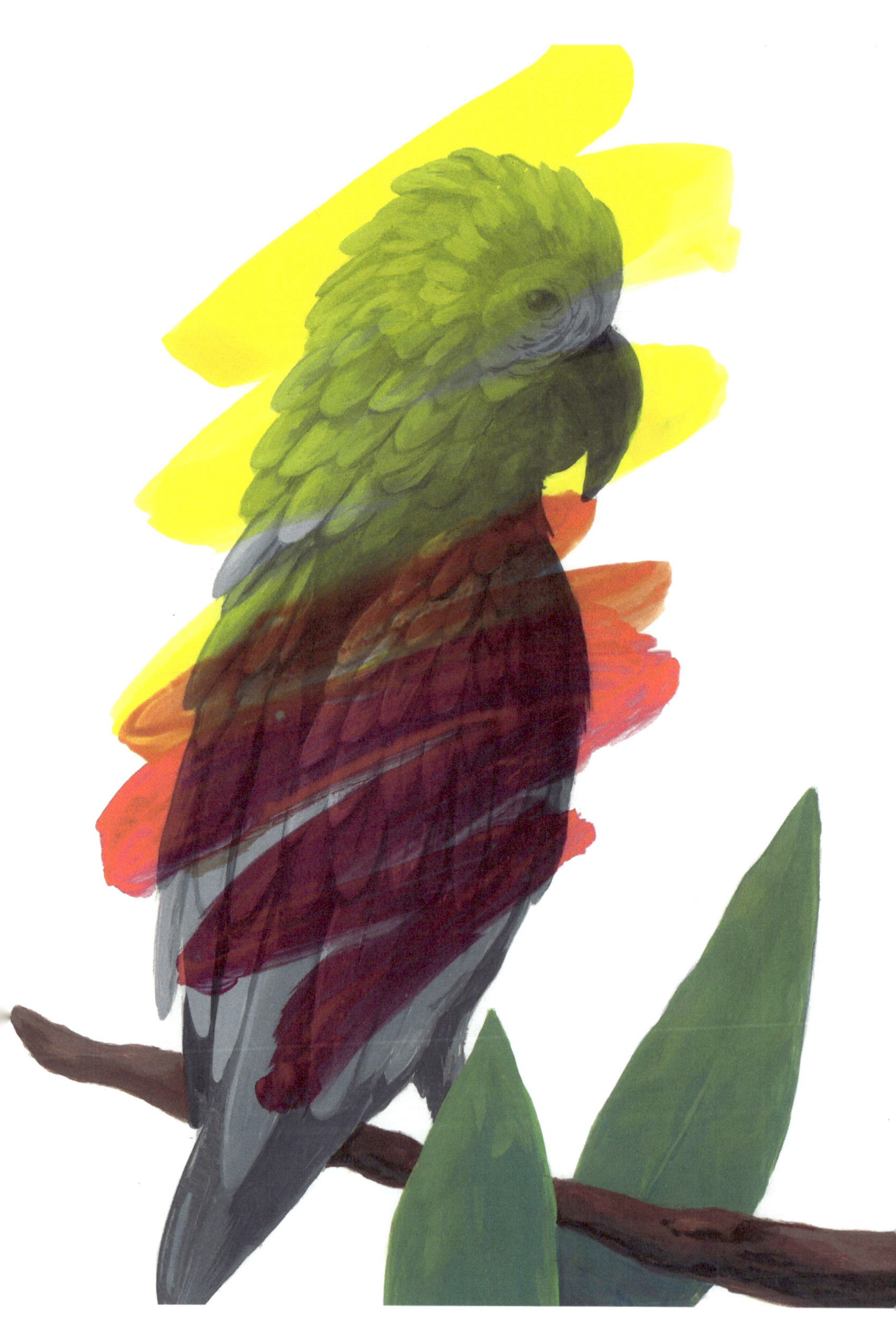

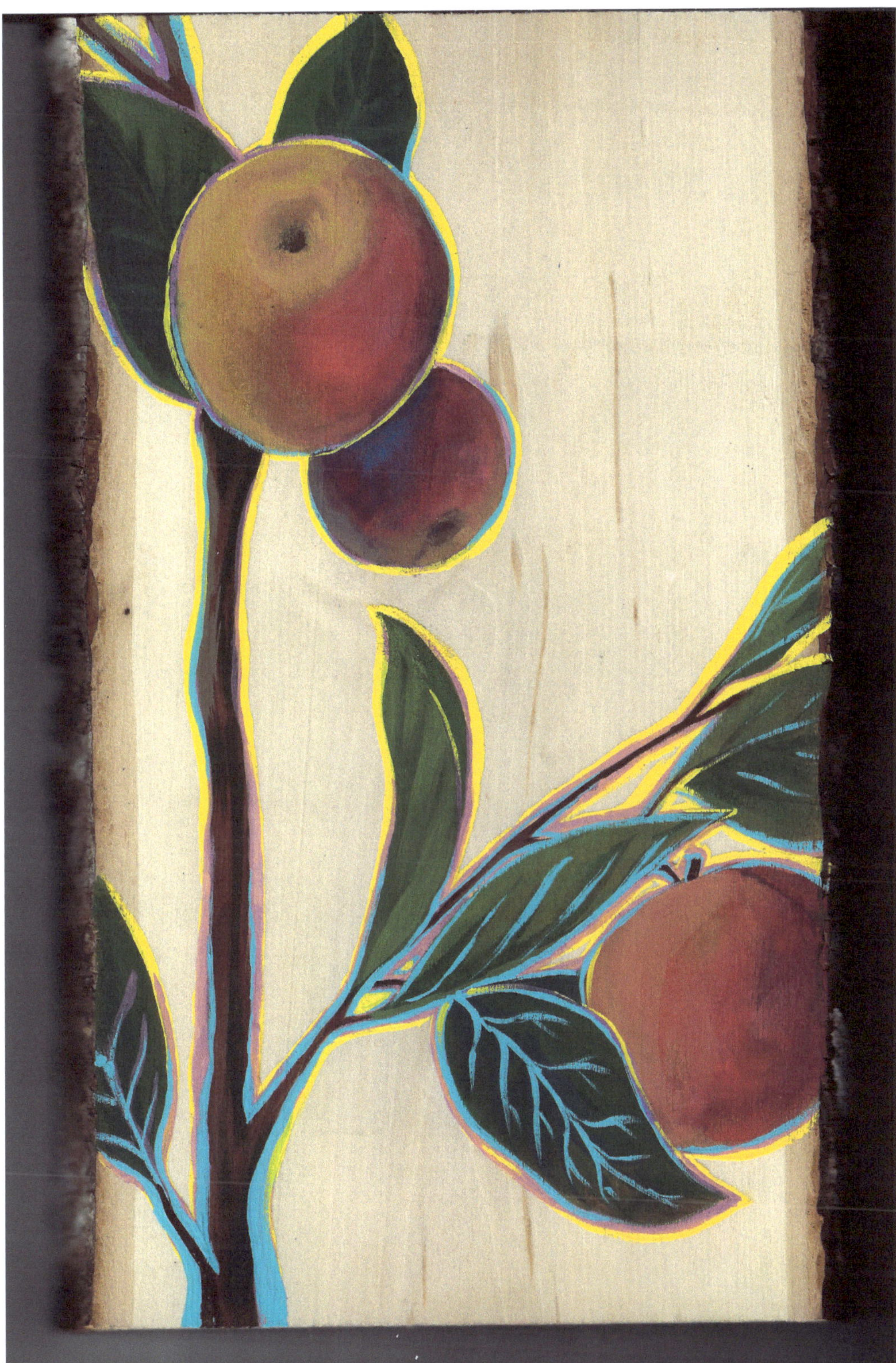

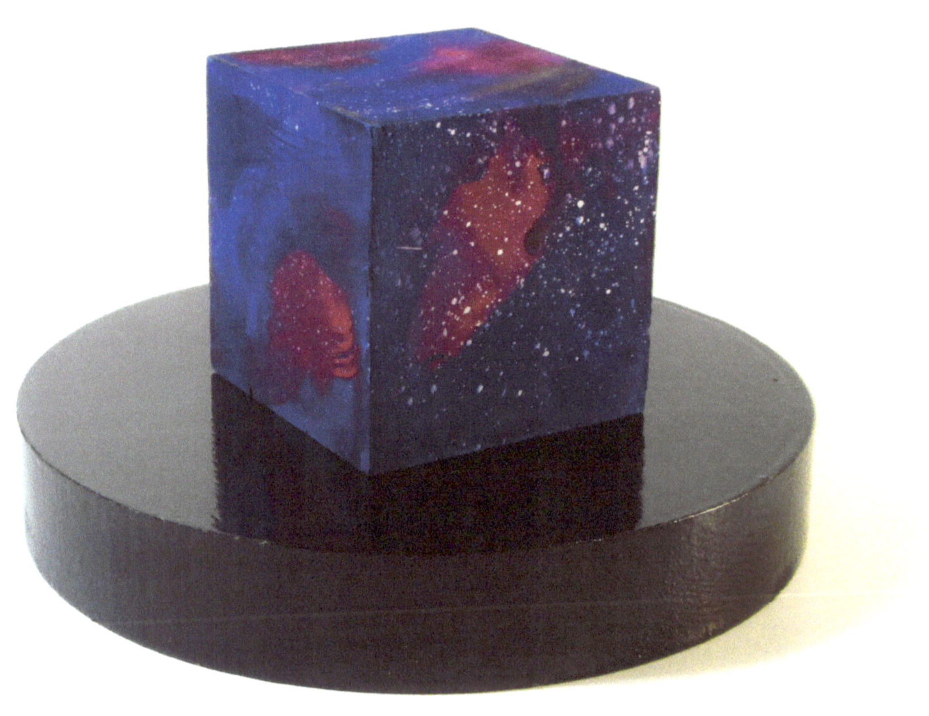

INHERITANCE

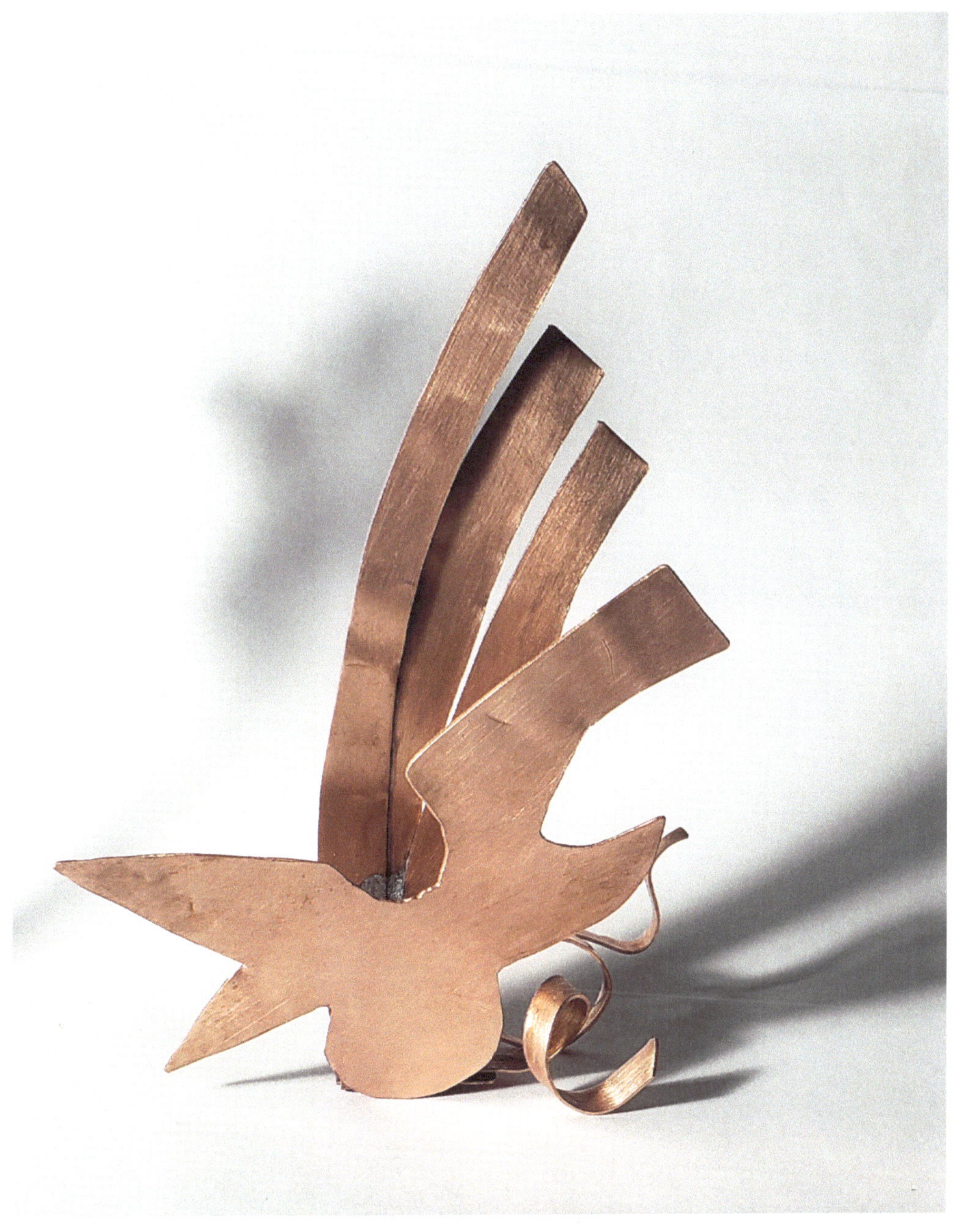

In early 2020 my uncle and fellow artist Walter Warren passed away. As a way of honoring him and expressing my gratitude for what he has done for me over the years, I completed small versions of sculptures he was planing in his sketchbook but never had the chance to finish.

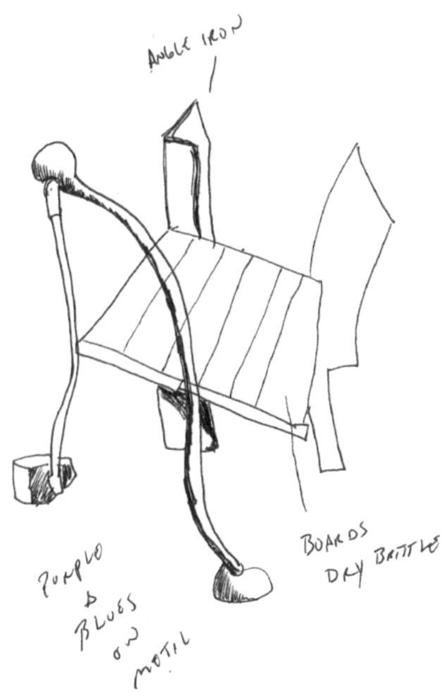

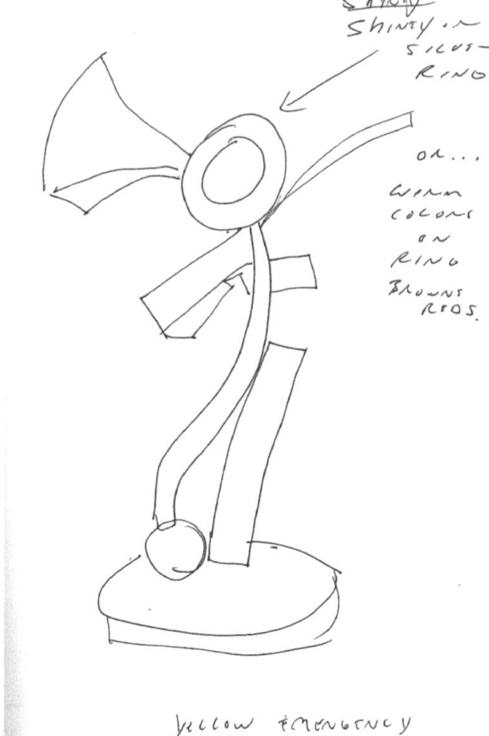

I PLAN ON WORKING WITH CHARCOAL THIS SUMMER IN BOTH (STILL LIFE, FIGURATIVE STUDIES. MAYBE THAT'S WHAT FUELS THE SUDDEN SURGE IN ARMS, HEADS, LEGS & TORSOS?

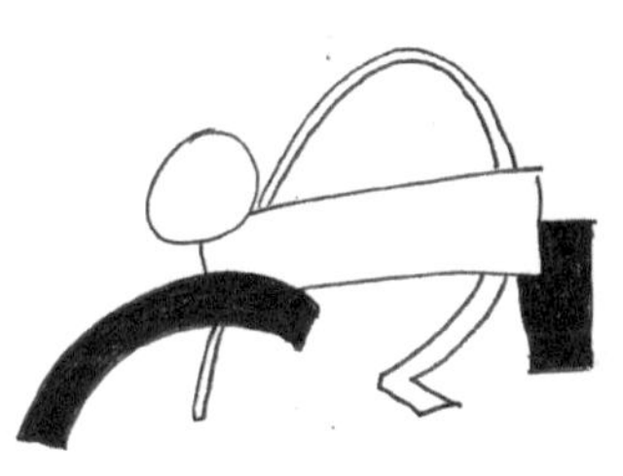

"I MISS SARAH"

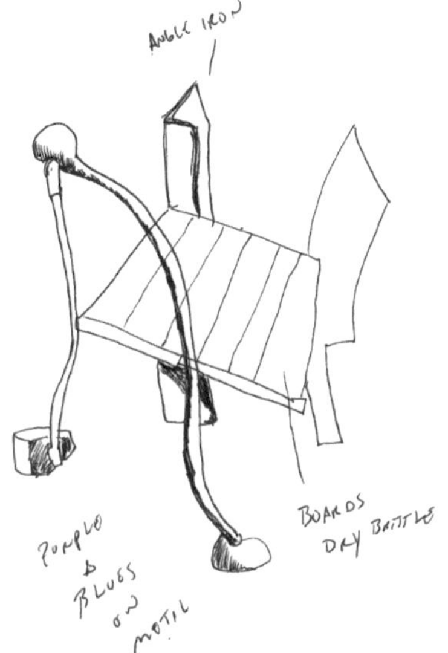

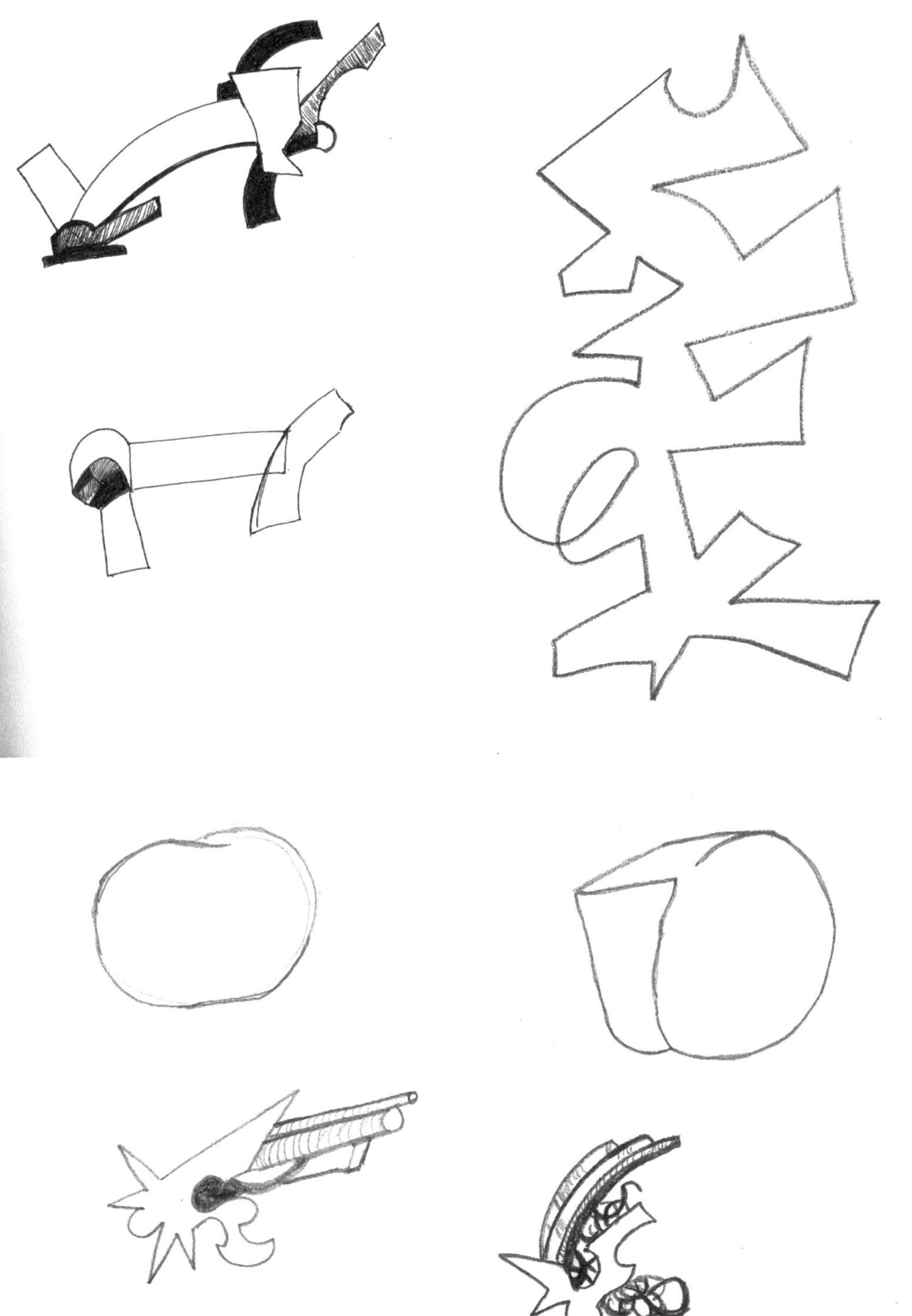

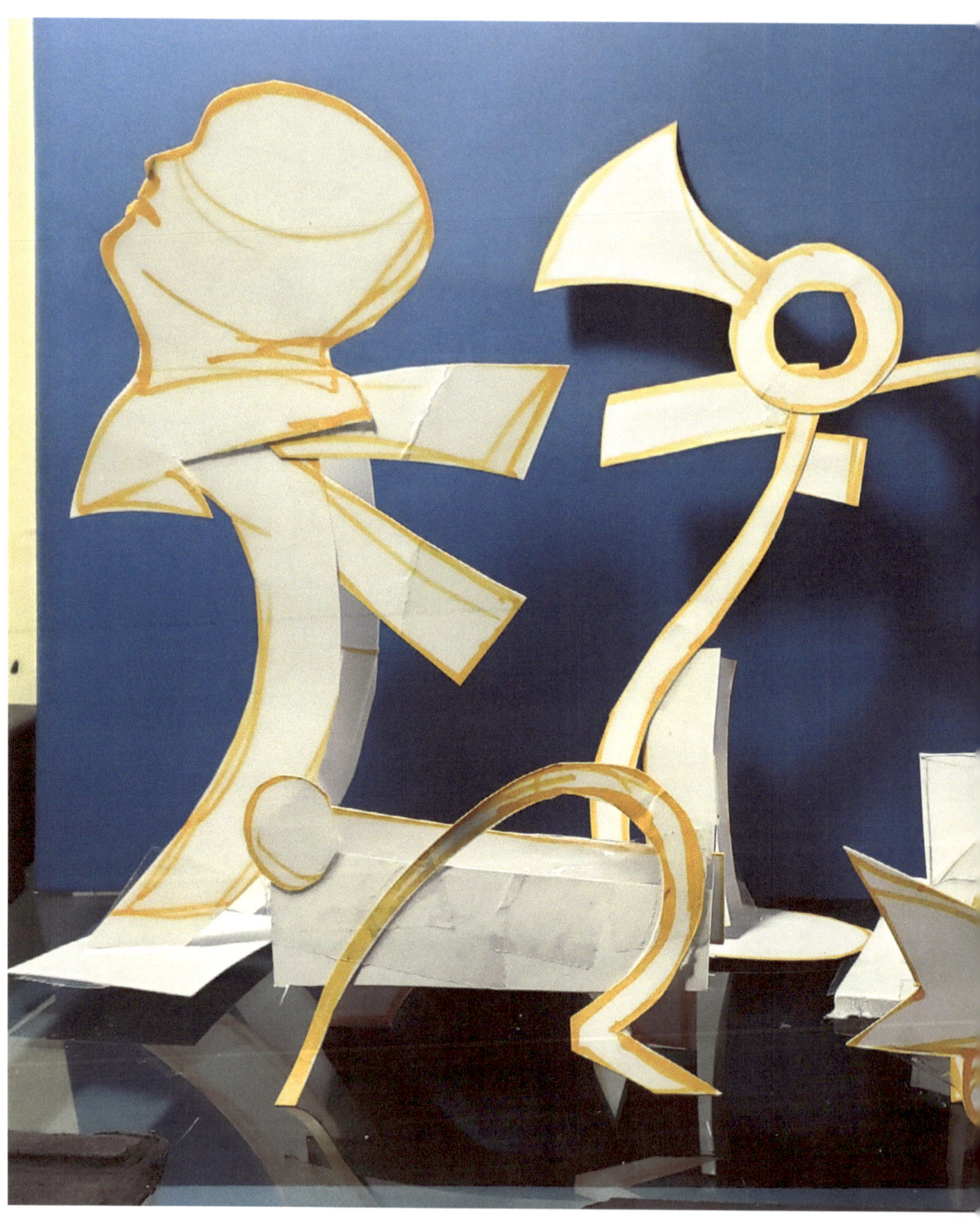

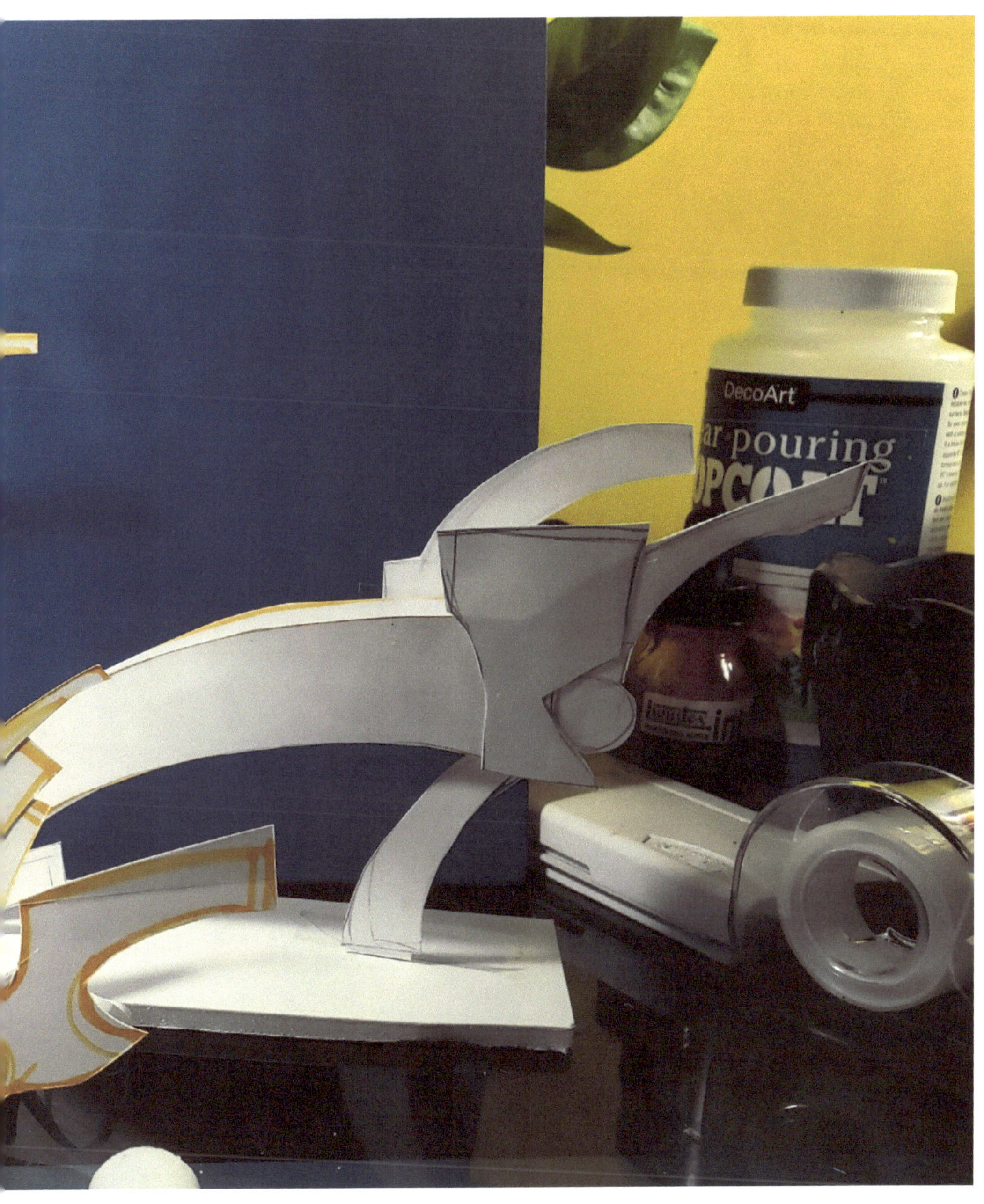
DecoArt
pouring

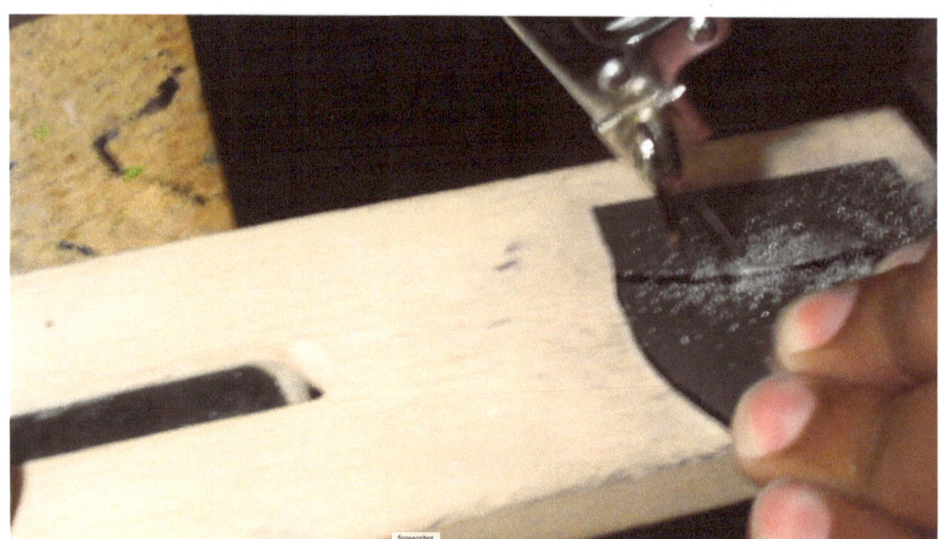
Screenshot

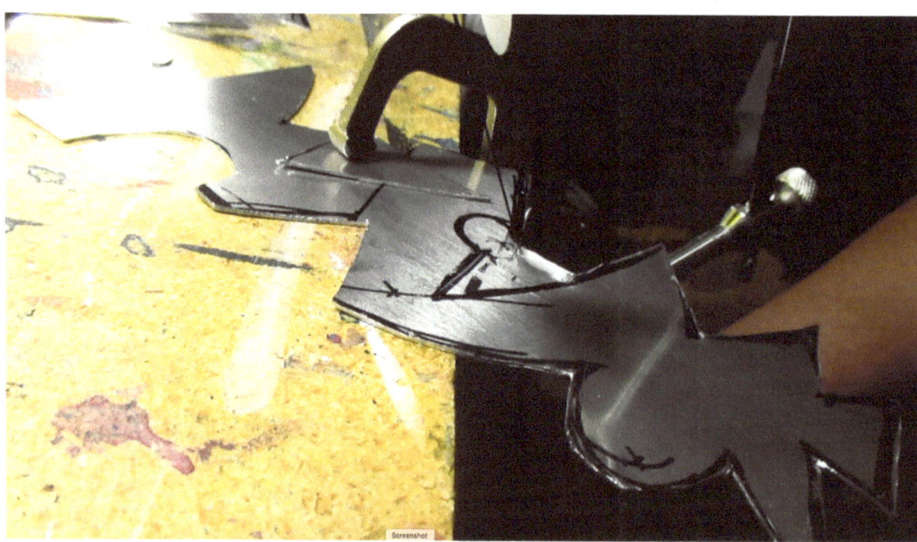
Screenshot

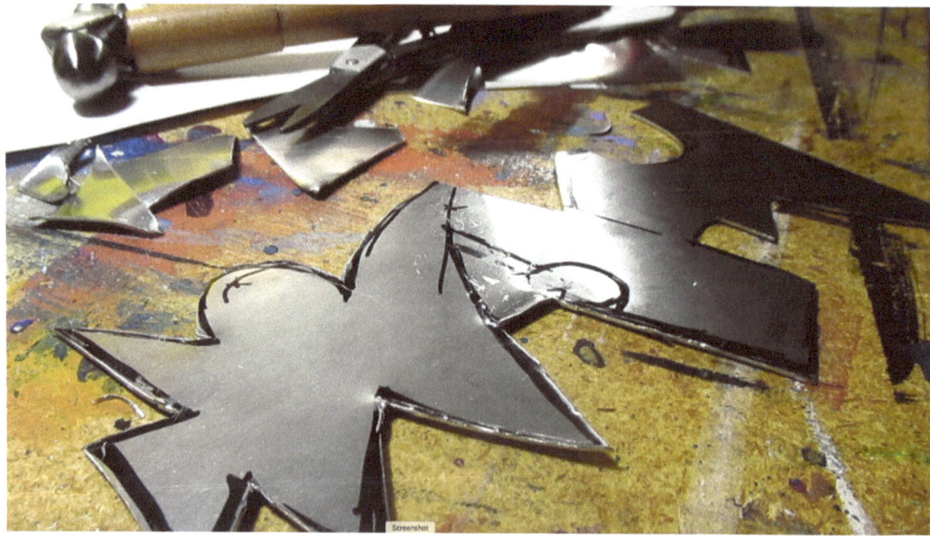
Screenshot

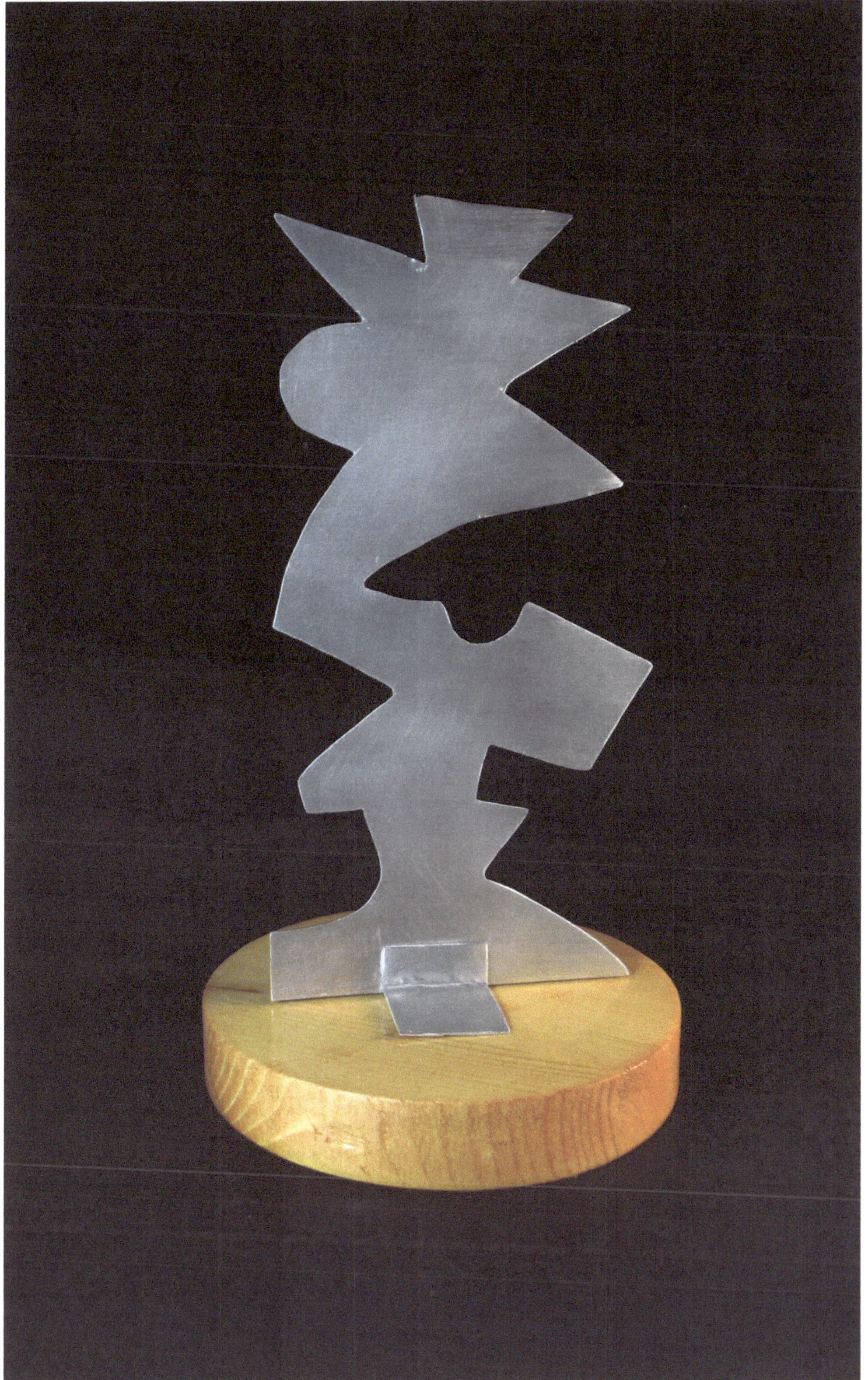

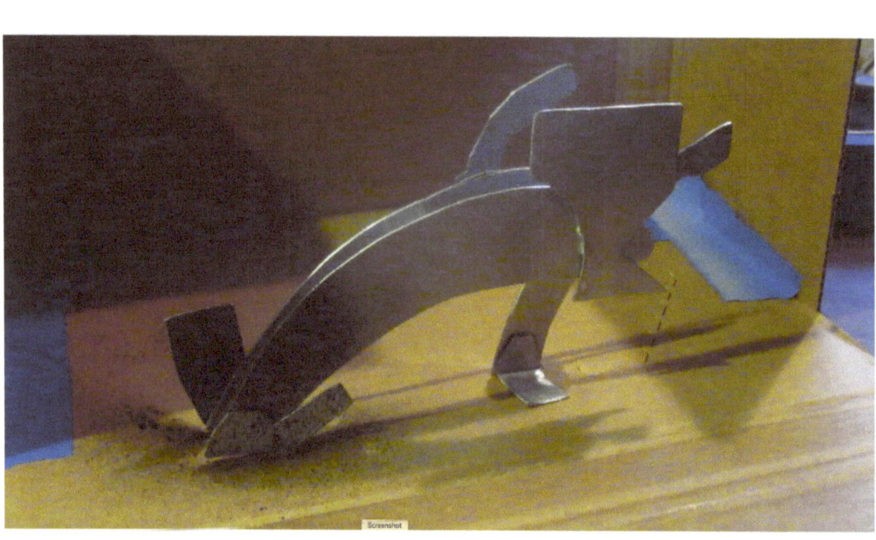

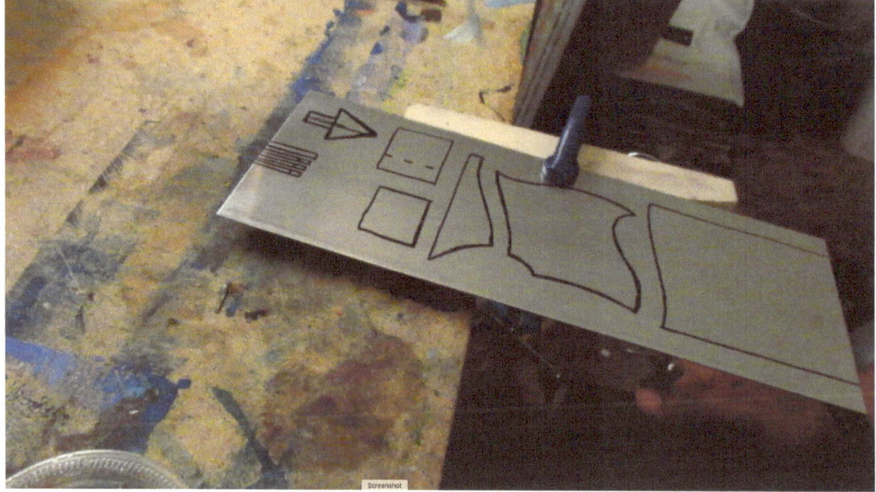

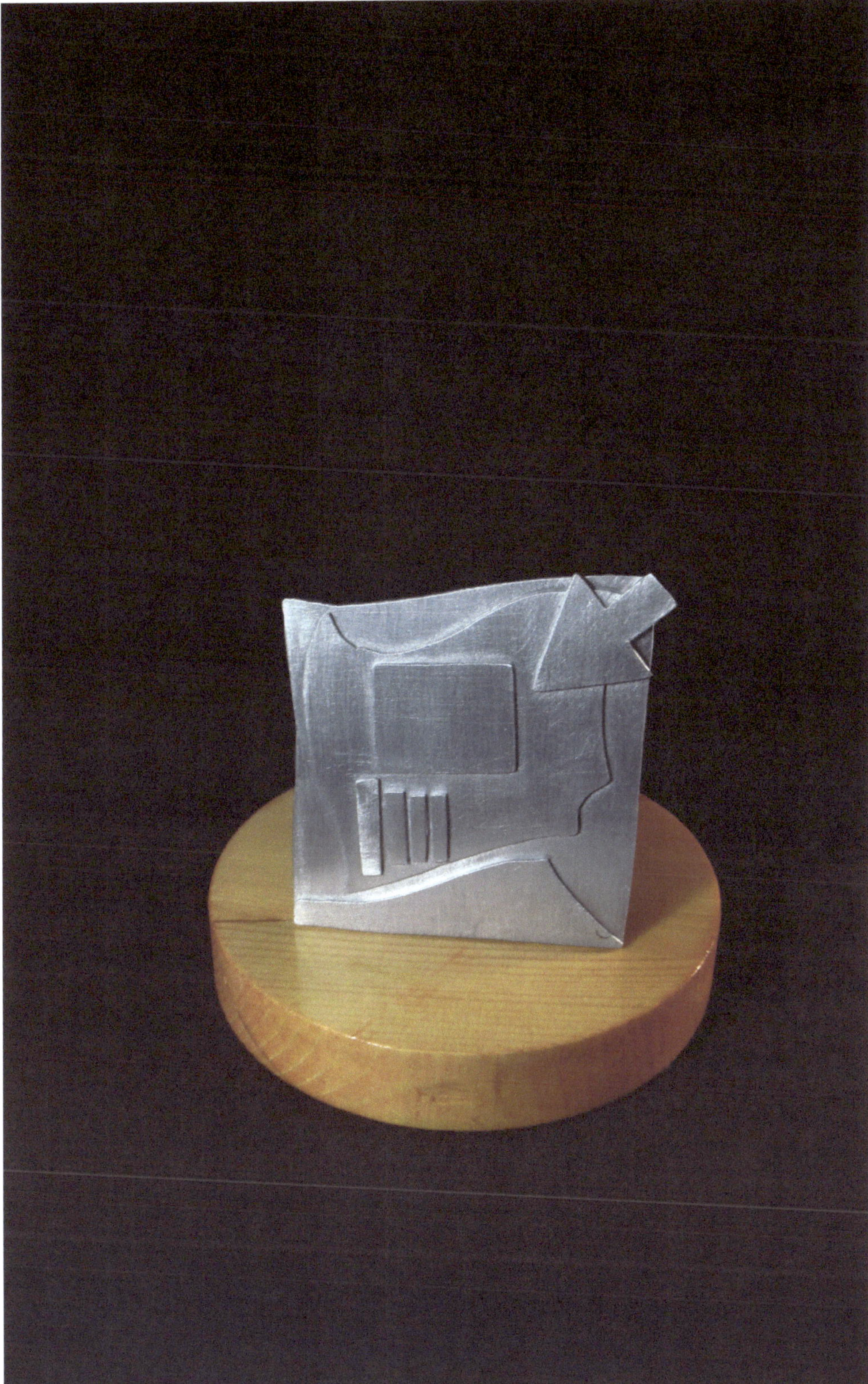

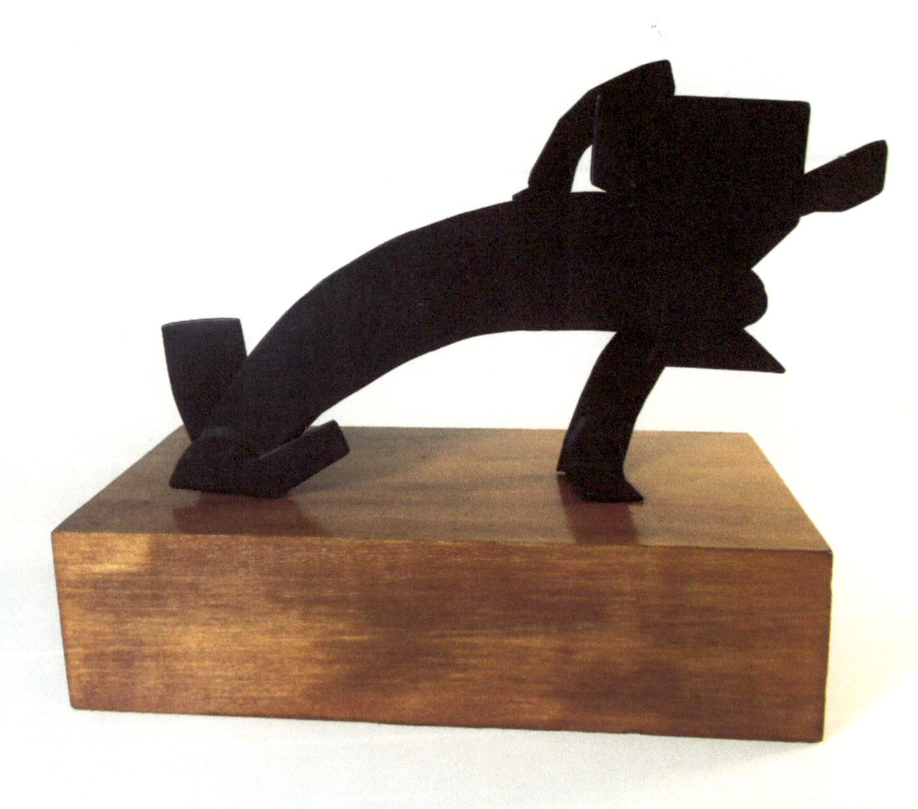

What is it I'm trying to accomplish? "the same old thing?" NO! I have grown a considerable amount since my last finished piece. I just haven't expressed myself in a three dimensional medium in some time.

Walter Warren

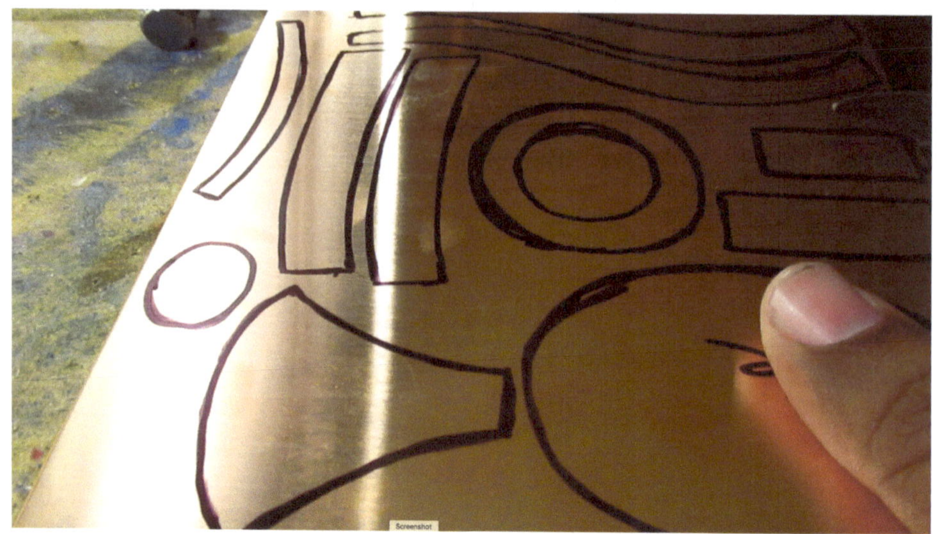

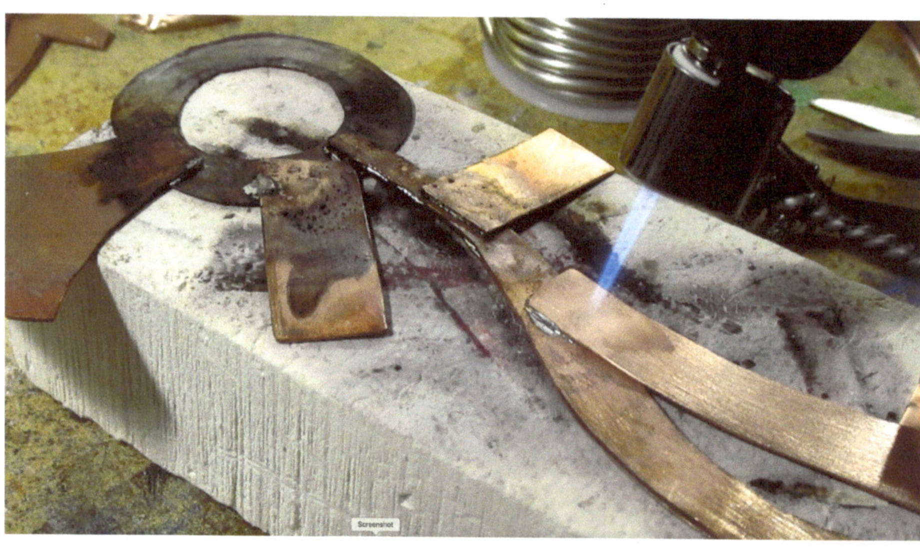

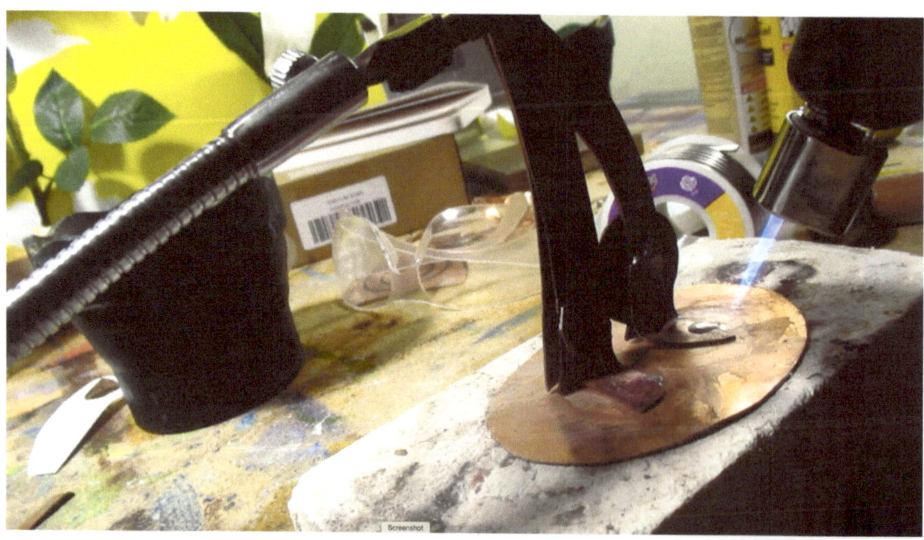

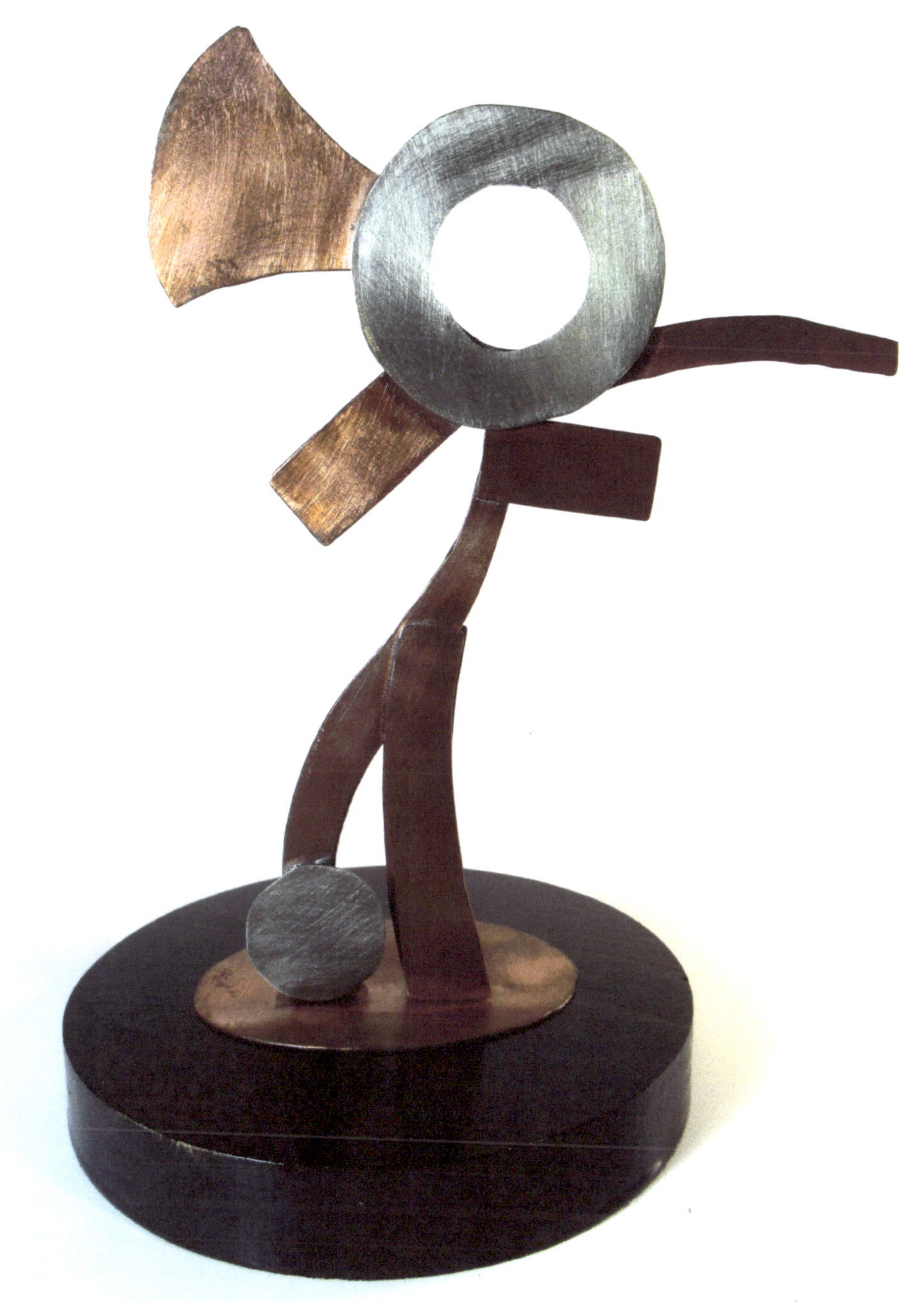

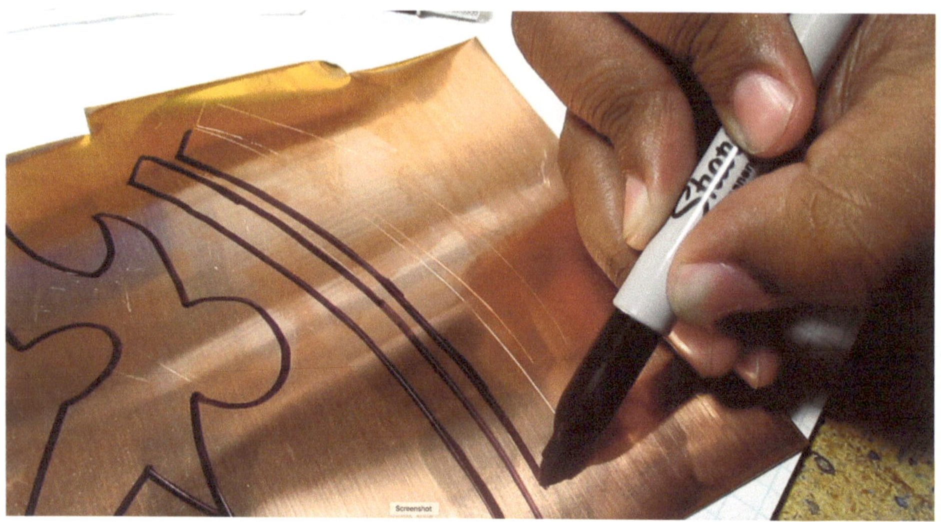

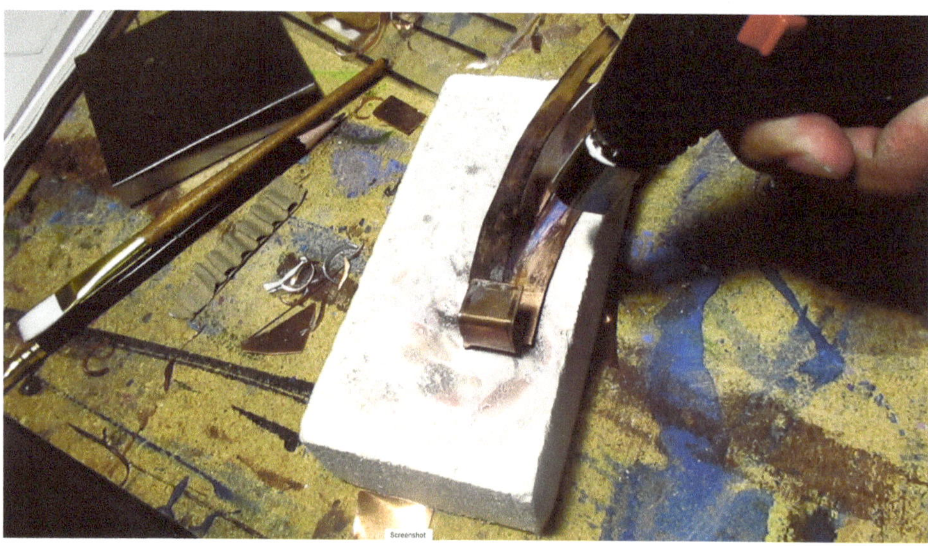

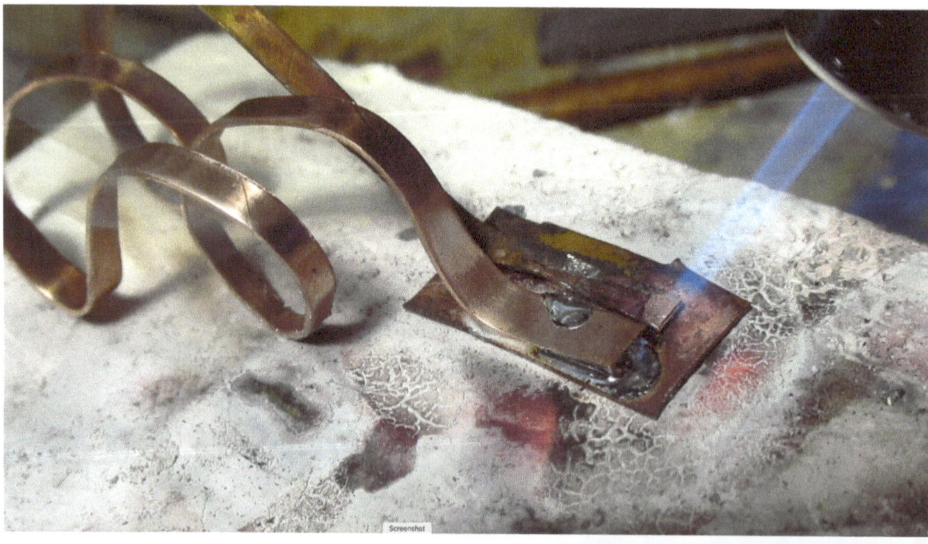

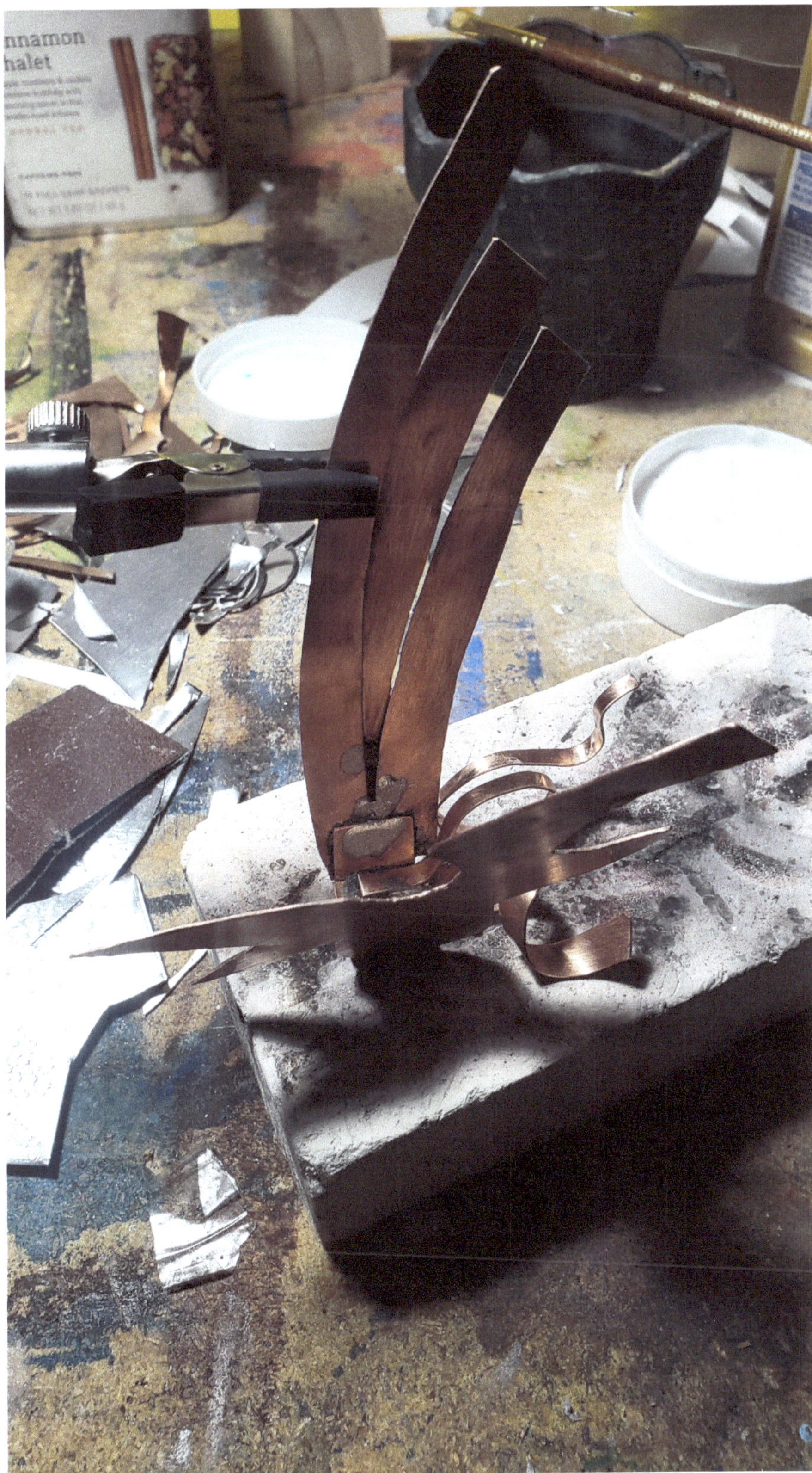

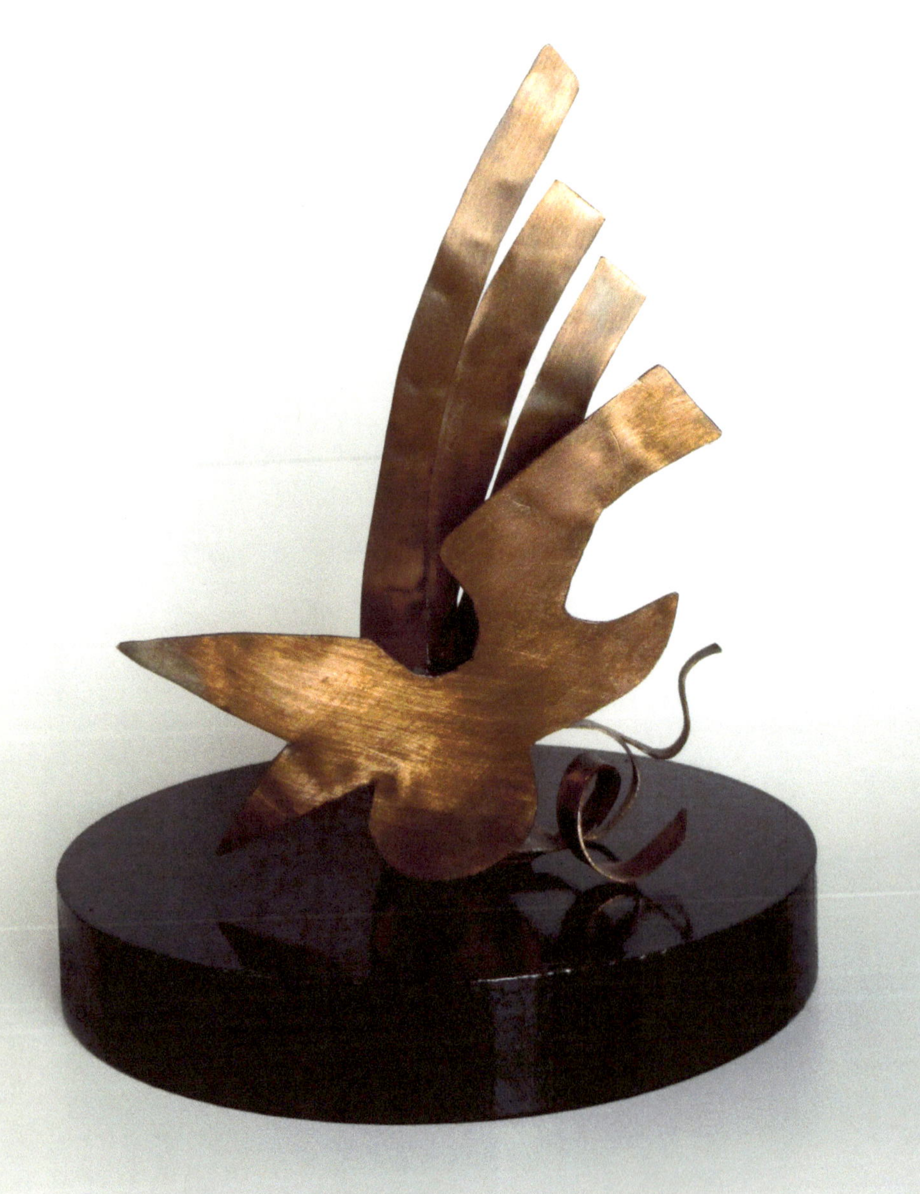

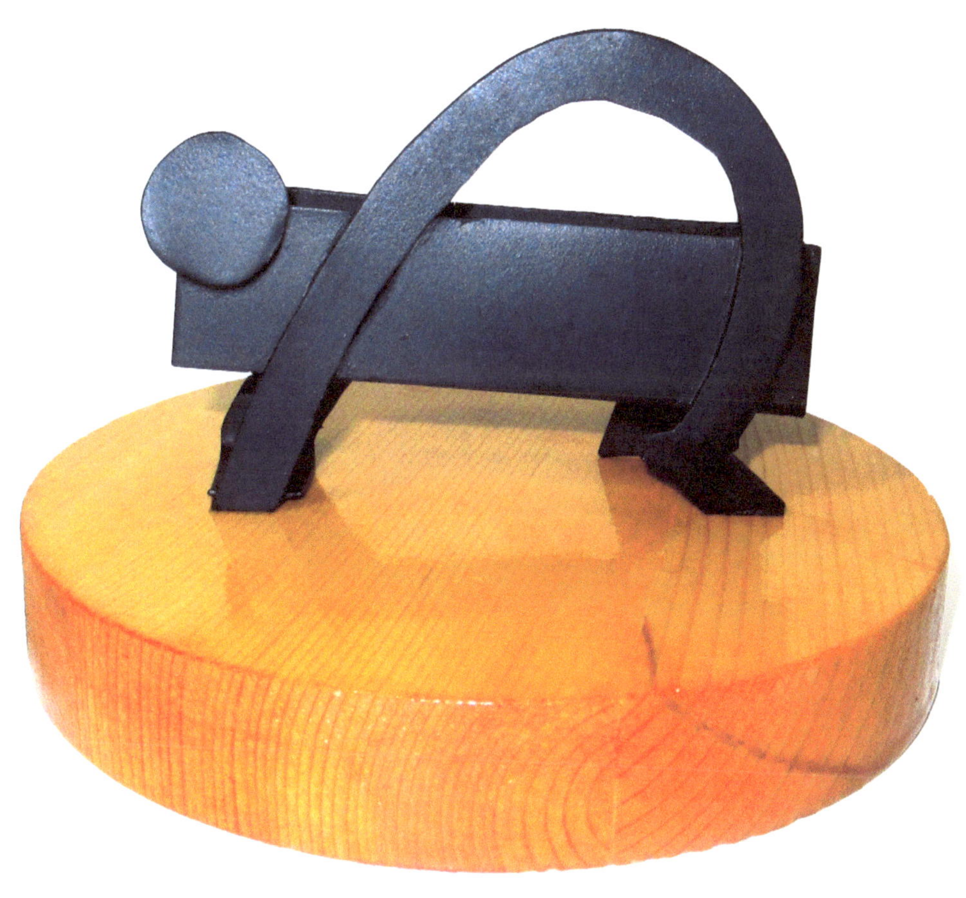

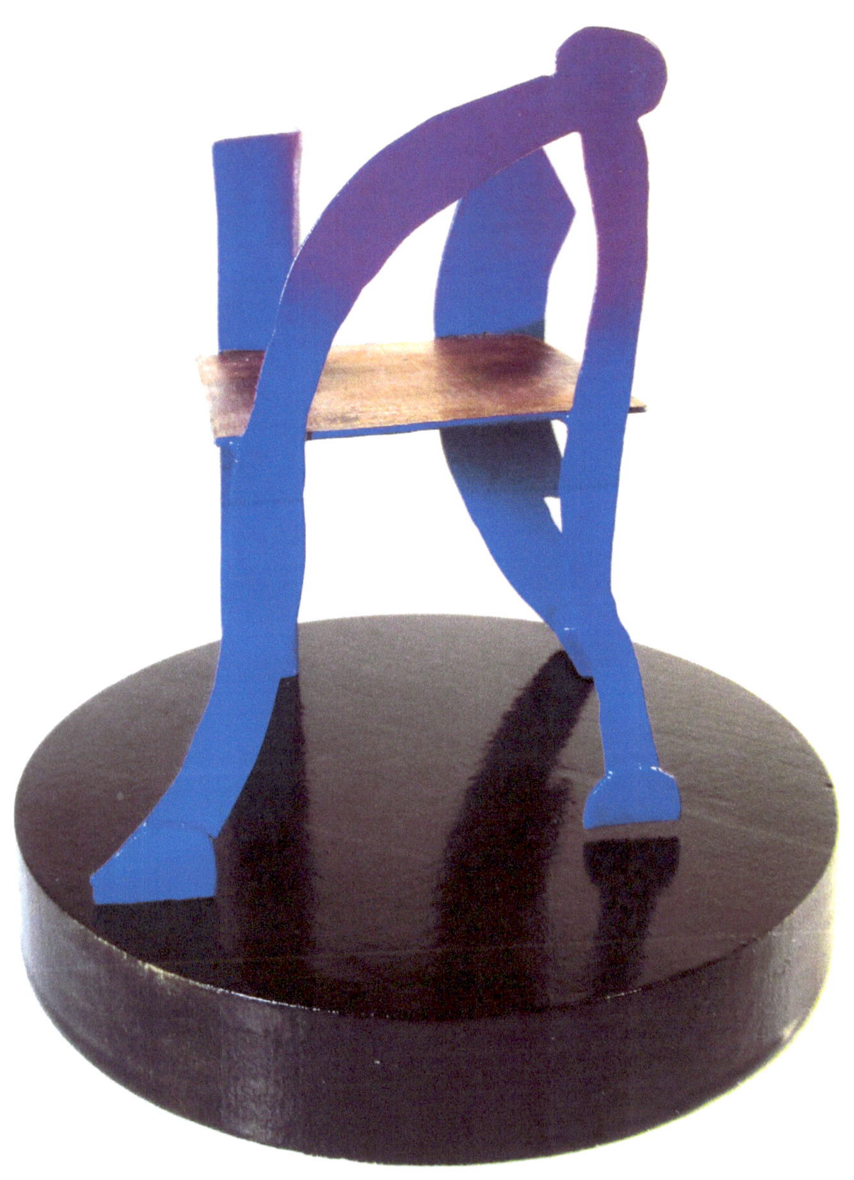

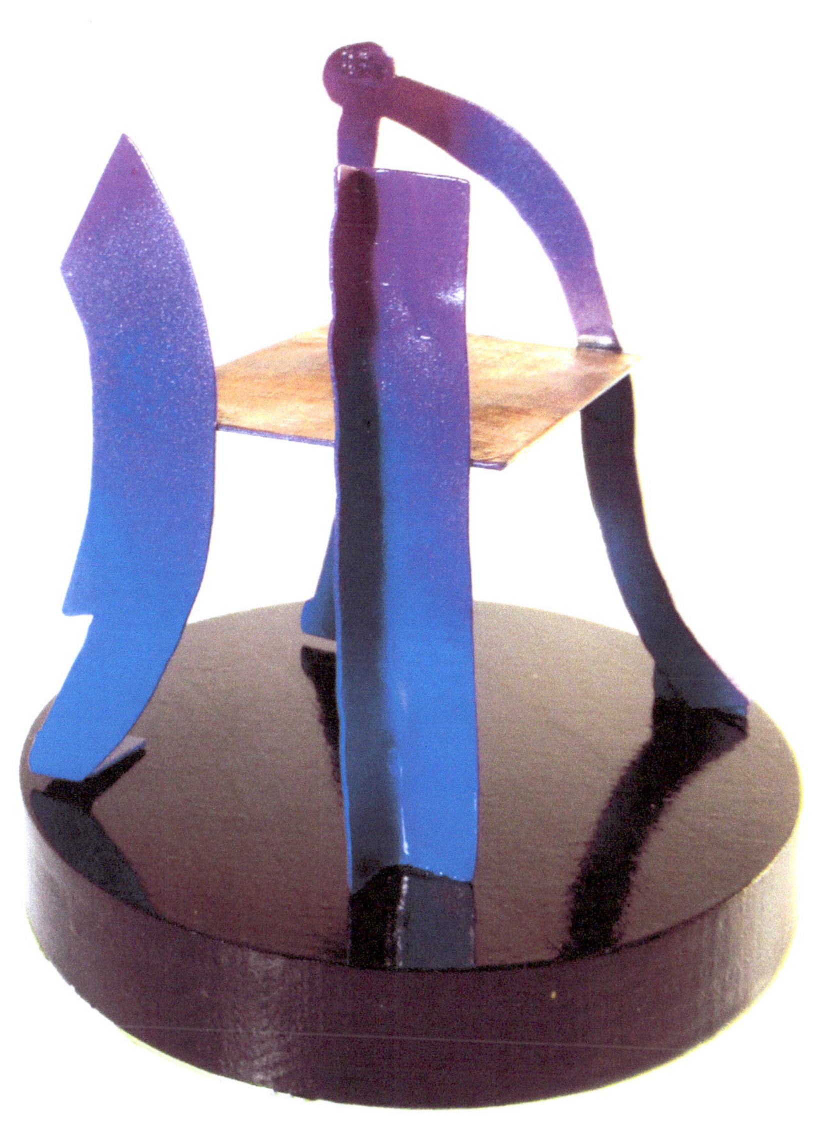

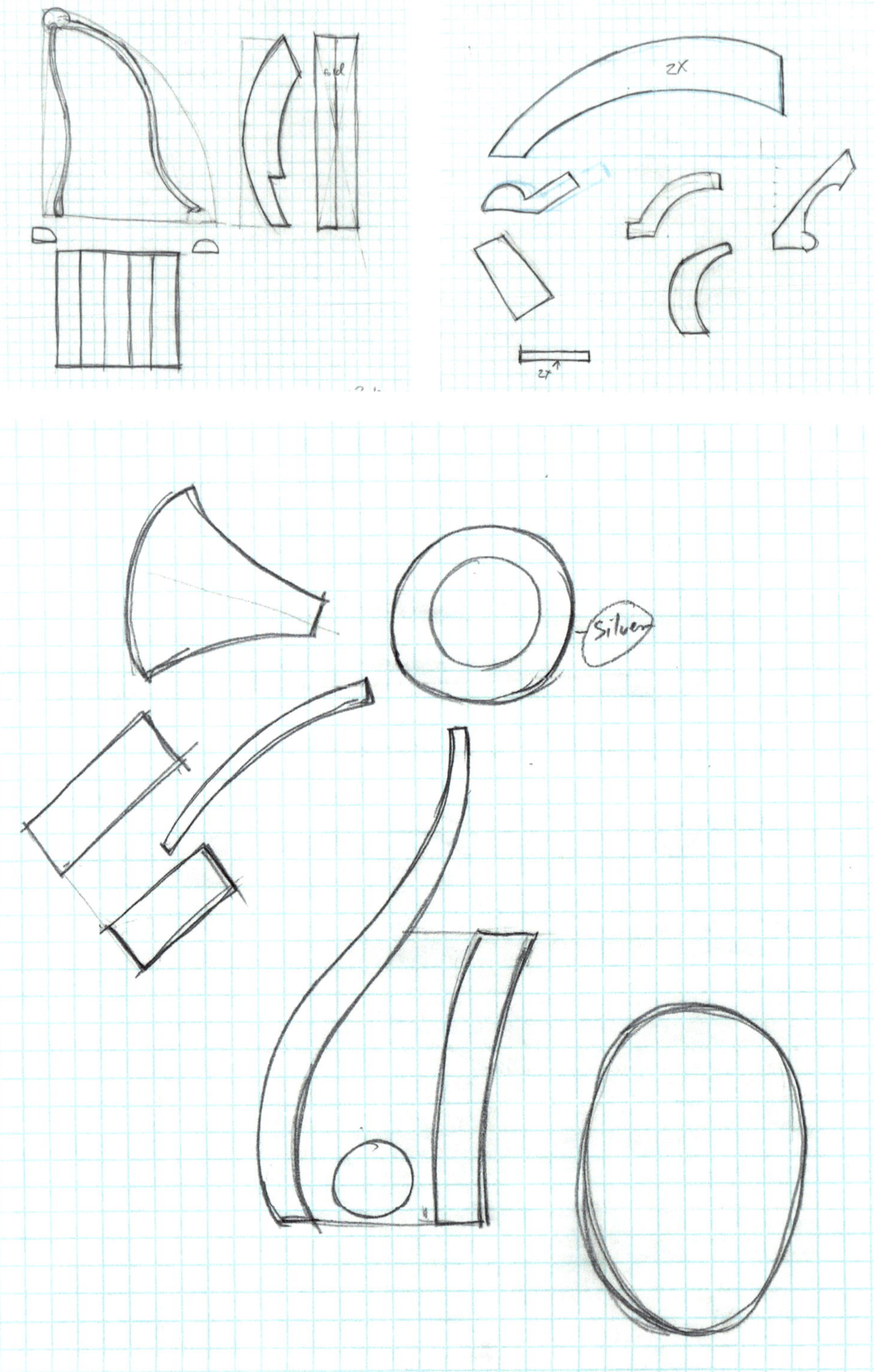
2X
Silver

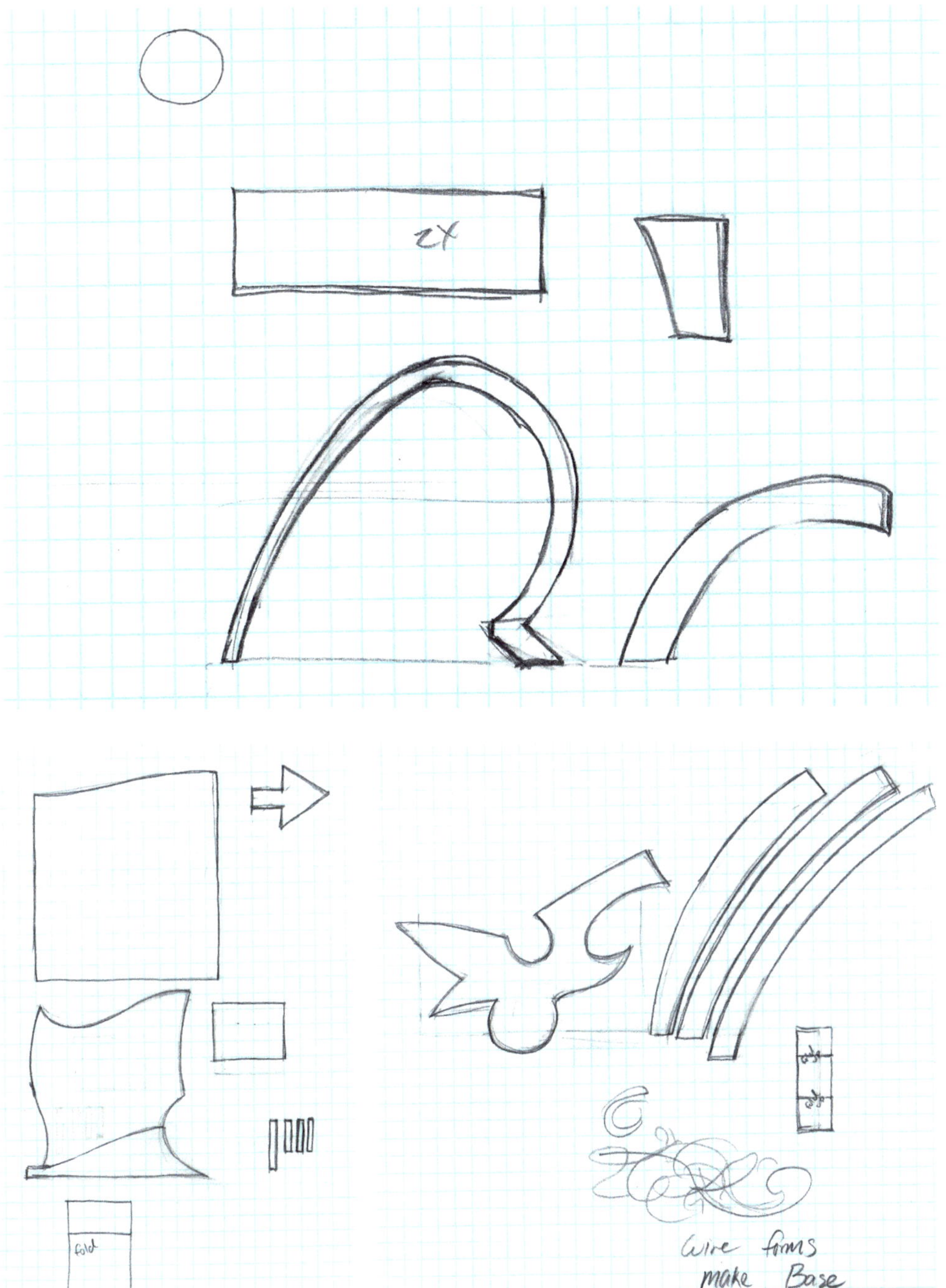
2X
fold
Wire forms
make Base

www.ingramcontent.com/pod-product-compliance
Lightning Source LLC
LaVergne TN
LVHW070239120826
845154LV00021B/115

9781736011003